Working with Black Children and Adolescents in Need

University of Chester
Warrington Campus

University of Chester Library
Tel: 01925 534284

Acknowledgements

This book owes much to the inspiration of Pat Massey, former Social Work Education Adviser, at the Central Council for Education and Training of Social Workers (CCETSW). I am grateful to her for her encouragement and support.

I would like to thank the contributors to this book for making time to put pen to paper to share their expertise with others. Special thanks are also due to Ratna Dutt, Jan Lord, Marcia Spencer and Shaila Shah for their helpful comments.

As ever, a special debt of gratitude is owed to my husband, Balbir, for his continual support and encouragement. Thanks Bir.

Working with Black Children and Adolescents in Need

Edited by
Ravinder Barn

British
Agencies
for **A**doption
and **F**ostering

Published by
British Agencies for Adoption & Fostering
(BAAF)
Skyline House
200 Union Street
London SE1 0LX

Charity registration 275689

Reprinted 2001

**British Library Cataloguing in Publication
Data**
A catalogue record for this book is available
from the British Library

ISBN 1 873868 71 5

Designed by Andrew Haig & Associates
Editorial project management by Shaila Shah
Cover illustration by Andrew Haig
Typeset by Avon Dataset Ltd, Bidford on Avon
Printed by Russell Press Ltd. (TU),
Nottingham

For Gulzaar and Arjun

Contents

Glossary

Asian – The term Asian is used to refer to those of South Asian background, who themselves or whose ancestors originate from the Indian Sub-continent.

Black – The term black is used in its political context to refer to those who share a common, but not necessarily similar, experience on the basis of their "race", colour and ethnic origin in Britain. In this book, it refers to individuals of African-Caribbean, Asian, African, and mixed parentage origin. Ethnic distinctions are made wherever necessary and relevant. Also, the term "minority ethnic" is used interchangeably with black.

Looked after – The term looked after refers to children in local authority care who are accommodated with parental or child consent and those in care following court proceedings. The terms "in care", and "in the public care system" are also used by different authors to refer to children looked after by local authorities.

Mixed parentage – Mixed parentage is used to refer to individuals of mixed racial and cultural origins. In this book, it is mostly used to refer to children with a white indigenous mother and an African-Caribbean/ African father. Other terms used by different authors to signify the same meaning are "mixed heritage" and "dual heritage".

Race – The word "race" is placed in inverted commas to stress that the categorisation of people into different "races" is a social definition – one which has been used to determine hierarchies which have dis-advantaged black people. It is not a biological definition as there is only one race, the human race. It is used here in the absence of a suitable alternative.

White – The term white is used to refer to both white indigenous and white European people.

Introduction

Ravinder Barn

There is a general paucity of literature in the area of direct work with black children "in need". Research evidence continues to document the high numbers of black children in the public care system, or at risk of abuse and neglect. Practitioners frequently voice the lack of available literature on the emotional and psychological needs of these children. This book aims to address that gap by focusing upon black children and adolescents in need. It is based on the premise that the onslaught of racism may mean that some black children and adolescents grow up with a distorted view of themselves, which is highly pejorative and self-denigrating.

Bhate and Bhate (1996) argue that communication difficulties can be one of the principal barriers to meeting the needs of black children. They describe these difficulties as primary (that is, arising out of the client's limited ability to speak or comprehend English) or secondary (difficulties due to cultural differences between client groups and professionals). Garbarino and Stott (1992) highlight the impact of the child's familial and cultural background upon their interaction and performance in an assessment situation with practitioners. Moreover, they argue that the practitioner's age, sex, ethnic background and degree of intrusiveness will affect the child's performance.

The Children Act 1989, for the first time in the history of British child care legislation, places emphasis upon the need for social workers to consider a child's racial, cultural, religious and linguistic background (Section 22(c), Children Act 1989) when making decisions about children they are looking after. Communicating with the child to obtain his/her views is deemed to be of crucial significance.

To adequately meet the social and psychological needs of black children, agencies must examine existing policies and practice and begin to recognise the particular context and background of the black child.

Thus, a focus upon needs arising out of the child's religious persuasion, cultural and linguistic background, and racial origin is paramount. Mehra (1996) identifies four major areas to begin to meet the emotional, psychological, religious, physical and social needs of the black child separated from their birth parents:

- To develop a positive identity for him/herself as a minority ethnic child.
- To develop the necessary linguistic, cultural, religious and social skills to function effectively as an adult in a multiracial and multicultural society.
- To acquire skills to cope as both child and adult in a society in which the child is likely to encounter racism, prejudice and disadvantage.
- To enable the child to come to terms with living apart from his/her birth family.

(Mehra 1996:80)

The ability to communicate effectively in these circumstances when assessments are being made is crucial. The Children Act 1989 places a great deal of emphasis upon communication and assessment. A welfare checklist is provided under the legislation (Children Act 1989, section 1(3)) which requires that the following be taken account of:

(a) the ascertainable wishes and feelings of the child concerned (according to the child's age and understanding)
(b) the child's physical, emotional and educational needs
(c) the likely effect on the child of any change in circumstances
(d) the child's age, sex, background and any characteristic that the court considers relevant
(e) any harm the child has suffered, or is at risk of suffering
(f) how capable each of the child's parents, and any other person in relation to whom the court considers the question to be relevant, is of meeting the child's needs
(g) the range of powers available to the court under this Act in the proceedings in question.

Consultation with children to find out their views is considered essential. So communicating with children to ascertain what they think, feel and need is of great importance. Methods employed to do this are many and varied. However, given their Eurocentric base, can they be applied for effective communication with black children? An adaptation of methods of working to incorporate the racial and cultural dimension is necessary.

The anti-racist movement within the social work profession in the 1980s played a significant role in raising issues about the needs and concerns of black users of social services. However, its focus upon Eurocentric models of working as inappropriate has had limited effect. There is an absence of an adequate conceptual framework, a framework that could and should encompass issues of "race" and ethnicity. Such a framework raises several questions:

- Do workers need to be armed with a catalogue of cultural practices of the black communities?
- What should or should not be encompassed under culture – festivals, family beliefs, attitudes and norms, religious rituals?
- How helpful is such a static and absolute view of culture?
- Where does the homogeneity of the black family and community fit into this?
- What of the individual and institutional racism perpetuated daily in this so called multiracial society?

There are a multitude of barriers that hinder effective communication between black children and adolescents and practitioners. Such barriers to effective cross-cultural communication include racism; cultural ignorance (negative stereotyping/cultural categorisation); inappropriate social work training; lack of suitable opportunities to develop racial and cultural competence, and language difficulties and misunderstandings. A recognition of the impact of "race" and racism upon black people in contemporary Britain, and an understanding of the evolving and dynamic nature of cultures is necessary amongst practitioners and carers.

The process of assessment and communication needs to take account of the adequacy and appropriateness of the theoretical basis for good practice. The importance of cultural relativism and issues of "race" and racism need to be given consideration to develop important strategies for empowerment. A paradigm shift where difference and diversity are positively recognised and the old framework of Eurocentrism is discarded is an essential prerequisite for working effectively with black children and adolescents.

A guide to the book

This anthology is intended for social work practitioners, carers, academics, trainers and students in social work. With its emphasis upon direct work with black children and adolescents in need, it raises important questions and considerations in developing appropriate antiracist strategies. The need to formulate an overall understanding of the impact of "race" and racism, and for antiracist and antidiscriminatory practices to be embedded into this, is crucial.

This collection offers practice-based suggestions for improving strategies and techniques of working with black children and young people. One common thread running throughout this book is that workers need to adopt a diversified approach and avoid the dangers of a narrowly focused reductionist perspective of "race" and culture.

Contributors – most of whom are black practitioners/carers with experience of working with black children – put forward suggestions for effective communication techniques, and argue that cultural and structural aspects are important considerations. This is also reinforced by the one contributor who is not a practitioner but was adopted as a child. The impact of cultural ignorance in the form of negative stereotyping and cultural categorisation is also discussed. It is argued that both black and white practitioners and carers need to address several aspects of their practice and develop ways of working with black youngsters.

Chapter 1 explores issues around racial and ethnic identity. In a society in which racial discrimination and disadvantage are everyday realities for minority ethnic groups, it is argued that the development of a positive identity based on religious, cultural, racial and linguistic aspects is crucial. The fluidity of the notion of identity is discussed to warn against crude stereotypes of "race" and ethnicity. The chapter also critically evaluates research evidence on racial identity within the context of transracial placements of black youngsters.

In Chapter 2, Nick Banks offers some useful strategies and techniques for working with black children. He puts forward a framework of assessment to distinguish different stages of identity work necessary.

Banks uses case study examples to illustrate difficult areas which can and do arise in undertaking identity work. The author also cautions against conceptualising and carrying out identity work in isolation from other identified needs of the child.

Chapter 3 tackles the area of early education and development of self-concept and identity in pre-school children. Alice Sawyerr provides an account of work undertaken in one nursery setting in inner-city London to illustrate important areas of consideration for workers and carers.

The particular situation of mixed parentage children is explored in Chapter 4. Beverley Prevatt Goldstein focuses upon significant issues and concerns around self-esteem, self-image and identity, and highlights some useful working strategies.

Bharti Dhir examines "race" and child protection in Chapter 5. The concept of "negative transferability", whereby negative feelings about self and own family are projected onto the ethnic group to which one belongs, is illustrated with practice examples. Useful suggestions of overcoming such negativity are discussed in the context of antidiscriminatory practice, and the importance of non-collusion with young people who may be denying their ethnic background is highlighted.

In Chapter 6, Aminah Husain Sumpton explores direct work with black children from a guardian *ad litem*'s perspective. (A guardian *ad litem* is a social worker who is appointed as the child's independent representative in care proceedings to inform the court about the child's wishes and feelings.) She focuses upon two case studies to illustrate the complexity of ethnicity incorporating the important dimensions of religion, culture, language and racial origin.

Michael Mallows presents an account of working with transracially adopted black youngsters in Chapter 7. He draws upon his current practice at the Post-adoption Centre in London, as well as intensive groupwork carried out on a residential outing in Wales to highlight issues for consideration for practitioners and adoptive parents.

Little is known about the educational needs of black children in the care system. By placing the discussion in a wider context of schooling, Toyin Okitikpi, in Chapter 8, argues that workers and carers should be more aware of the importance of education and the positive role it can play in the lives of looked after black children. He puts forward a perspective which challenges local authorities to give due consideration to the formal education of looked after children whilst meeting their other emotional and psychological needs.

Chapter 9 puts forward a black adoptive parent's perspective. Sally Baffour offers an understanding of her personal experience of adopting two young African children. She highlights difficulties encountered and gives an account of the adjustment period. The positive contributions of a black adoptive family are abundantly clear in this personal account.

In Chapter 10, Sue Jardine, transracially adopted as a child, outlines a personal account of her experiences of transracial placement. She writes openly and cogently about the pain and emotional turmoil presented in a transracial family setting. Drawing from her own experience as well as that of other transracial adoptees, Jardine offers practical suggestions to bring about positive changes in the lives of transracially adopted black young people.

Lynda Ince in Chapter 11 examines the experiences of black care leavers. She uses case study material from her own empirical research in this area to highlight issues and concerns affecting black care leavers.

It is hoped that this book will make a useful contribution to social work theory and practice on working with black children and adolescents.

References

Bhate, S. and Bhate, S. (1996) 'Psychiatric needs of ethnic minority children'. In (eds) Dwivedi, K. N. and Varma, V. P. *Meeting the Needs of Ethnic Minority Children*, London: Jessica Kingsley Publishers.

Garbarino, J. and Stott, F. M. (1992) *What Children Can Tell Us*, San Francisco: Jossey-Bass Publishers.

Mehra, H. (1996) 'Residential care for ethnic minority children'. In (eds) Dwivedi, K. N. and Varma, V. P. *Meeting the Needs of Ethnic Minority Children*, London: Jessica Kingsley Publishers.

1 Racial and ethnic identity

Ravinder Barn

Introduction

The concept of a racial and ethnic identity is an important one for all of us. Yet in the context of British society, identity as an issue has entered the world of academic and political debate only so far as black children are concerned. Nowhere is this more hotly contested than in the area of substitute family placements of black children. Such a framework generates a vacuous debate where the problems and concerns of black children are discussed with reference only to themselves (Gill and Jackson, 1983; Tizard and Phoenix, 1993) whilst issues around white children's identity are taken for granted as the unspoken norm.

In a society in which racial discrimination and disadvantage are an everyday reality for minority ethnic groups, the importance of an identity based on racial, cultural, religious and linguistic aspects is crucial. However, it is absolutely essential to recognise the fluidity of this notion of identity that is based on aspects which are themselves dynamic and evolving. For second, third and fourth generation black people living in Britain, identity has taken a different form at different times which may or may not be radically different from that of their parents and grandparents (Gilroy, 1987; 1993).

For black children growing up in an extremely race conscious society, where their cultural and religious origins are given little positive significance by wider society, the concept of a positive identity is paramount. It is only through appropriate integration into the child's experience that a positive and healthy identity can be formed. Small (1984) argued that if a healthy personality is to be formed, the psychic image of the child must merge with the reality of what the child actually is. Moreover, the black child must also be enabled to "transcend reality" if they are not to get engulfed and rendered impotent by such negative social images and possible feelings of personal impotence (Chestang, 1972). The children most likely to develop a positive "cognitive set" are those who, within the context of their own culture and relationships, have been exposed to 'secure, stable, affectional relationships, and experiences of success and achievements' (Rutter, 1985).

The operationalisation of identity

The psychological concept of identity is an elusive one. When "race" and culture are added to the equation, the academic debate becomes even more complex. Indicators for its measurement are highly subjective and value-laden. Researchers or other observers who attempt to comment on this are invariably accused of either racial vacuousness, or political and ideological dogma (Barn, 1994).

Much has been written about "identity confusion", "culture conflict", "low self-esteem", and a supposed poor image of the black child. Writers from various theoretical standpoints have theorised about the black child's self-concept. Academic debate has focused on a number of important areas, namely "home and family life", "the education system" and "the public care system". It is undeniable that the pernicious nature of racism in British society takes its toll in all spheres of black people's lives. However, an acceptance of these pathological models of and theories about black children lends credence to arguments that portray "race" as a biological entity to explain differences between people (Herrnstein and Murray, 1994). It is vital to recognise the structural processes at work, which do much damage. Whilst it is crucial to acknowledge that some black children will experience difficulties, black children, on the whole, must not be perceived as objects of pity, as pathological beings who are experiencing grave psychological problems. Such a framework that labels an entire group as a problem is oppressive and highly problematic in itself.

There is no doubt that children born and brought up in any society will take and make use of some ideas and certain values of the dominant culture in which they live. However, it is equally true that parental values and ideals also play an influential role in the lives of young people. It has been argued that the black family, institutions, and community can serve as conduits of the negative messages from white society and as sources for alternative frames of reference and significant others for black children and adults (Taylor, 1976; Barnes, 1981).

Moreover, the cultural forms that develop are not merely the result of a relationship between the host country and the migrant worker but are evolving entities influenced by the global culture. Needless to say, there are issues of power and domination in the value and meaning accorded to cultures. Gilroy (1987) argued that British black people define themselves as part of a diaspora, and consequently are culturally inspired by black populations elsewhere in the world. They adapt these other cultures to their own British experience and meaning, thereby creating and re-creating their own unique cultural identities.

Transracial placements and identity
For over three decades, black children being looked after by local authority social services departments have been placed in transracial settings, that is, in white substitute families. White children have not had to experience similar upheaval at a time of separation and loss from the birth family. Cheetham (1981) found that social workers were reluctant to place white children in black families even when such families were available.

Black children's best interests were perceived from political and ideological perspectives to the detriment of many such children who have had to grow up in a racial and cultural vacuum. The historical background of the "melting pot" philosophy which believed that racial integration was best achieved by taking black children into white homes has been discussed elsewhere (Rhodes, 1992; Barn, 1993).

Since the early 1980s, the negative and highly disturbing experiences of black children in transracial settings have come to light (Gill and Jackson, 1983; Divine, 1983; BIC, 1984). In the context of a transracial setting, it was noted that the denial of the reality of the black child in a white family or environment would eventually create identity confusion/conflict in that child (Small, 1984). Indeed, research studies of black children in white substitute families who are isolated from black communities have demonstrated that these children have failed to develop a positive racial identity (Gill and Jackson, 1983). Research studies into intercountry adoptions in the United States have painted a similarly bleak picture and have warned of the severe damage to a child's

9

racial and ethnic identity (Wilkinson, 1985; Koh, 1988). Many of these children have grown up believing or wishing themselves to be white, and have internalised the "white" values, norms and attitudes of significant others. Gill and Jackson (1983) recognised the identity confusion experienced when they stated that 'these black children have been made white in all but skin colour' (p 137).

Gill and Jackson (1983) made a study of the children in their adolescent years to explore this period of identity confusion (Erikson, 1968). The findings showed that the majority of the 36 study families were living in areas which were either entirely white or in which there was only a small proportion of black residents. Eighteen families had no black "friends of the family". Adoptive parents showed little appreciation of the child's culture, but expected the child to have an automatic pride in it. Gill and Jackson stressed that these parents adopted their children at a time when not highlighting their child's racial background was regarded as the appropriate approach. They stated that the way in which these parents were bringing up their children seemed consistent with the "melting pot" approach of the 1960s. With regard to children's perceptions of their ethnic origin, the researchers stated:

The evidence ... paints a picture of children who, although not directly denying their racial background, perceived themselves to be "white" in all but skin colour... There was little evidence of a positive sense of racial identity.

(Gill and Jackson, 1983:81)

Despite evidence to the contrary, Gill and Jackson presented their central argument as one of support for the continual practice of transracial placements:

... we feel confident in using the term "success" to describe the experience of the majority of these children.

(Gill and Jackson, 1983:132)

John Small, the then president of ABSWAP and former Assistant Director of Hackney Social Services, at an ABSWAP conference in 1983 argued that this designation of the adoptions as "successful" might come implicitly from an integrationist position so that the fact that the children did not see themselves as black was seen as good insofar as it facilitated the creation of a genuine multiracial society where "colour" is irrelevant. This suggests that the stance adopted by the researchers of this study is akin to that of the melting pot era of the 1960s. In their own words, Gill and Jackson stated that they did not want to:

. . . give undue emphasis to racial background or to emphasise the differences between parent and child.

(Gill and Jackson, 1983:13)

In their research design and interpretation of findings, Gill and Jackson adhered to a narrowly defined social class analysis whereby success is measured according to the child's middle class background and educational attainment. The ethnicity of the child is reduced to a level of non-significance. Much of their study revolved around the elusive concept of identity; identity was seen as something that exists almost in a vacuum. The research failed to move beyond the set parameters of identity to observe the wider impact of societal and global issues into "race" and ethnicity. There is little conceptualisation of the position of black people in British society except a passing remark which led one black practitioner to state that the research was 'defective, hypocritical, and patronising' (Divine, 1983). Having given no regard to the problems faced by black people throughout the research, Gill and Jackson stated in their conclusion:

Transracial adoption over the past two decades has illustrated and highlighted the disadvantages of blacks in white society . . . The black community has every justification for seeing itself as a "donor" of children for white couples. Such a perception can do little for the dignity and self-determination of that community. To have a system which through "benign neglect" in effect systematically removes black children from black homes and places them in white homes without any traffic in the opposite direction can hardly be beneficial for the black community.

(Gill and Jackson, 1983:137)

Divine (1983) argued that comments such as the one above are no more than mere lip service, and only serve to add to the hypocrisy of the researchers. He noted the damaging effect of the research on social work policy and practice:

> *Having relegated ethnic identity as an irrelevance which is the effect of not including it as one of the crucial ingredients to be noted in the "successful" placement of a black child, one cannot turn around and argue as an afterthought almost, about the "dignity" and "self determination" of the black community and expect child care agencies and our communities to take it seriously.*

(Divine, 1983:4)

The most notable finding of the Gill and Jackson study was that transracial placements are successful. Yet, in their conclusion, Gill and Jackson argued:

> *Nevertheless, in our view, there are strong arguments for saying that wherever possible black children needing a permanent substitute home should be placed in black rather than white families.*

(Gill and Jackson, 1983:139)

Considering the fact that Gill and Jackson rejected all the arguments put forward by the opponents of transracial placements and viewed such placements as successful, it is ironic that they recommended black families for black children. Their lack of explicit emphasis upon issues of "race" and ethnicity within their methodological framework and their subsequent interpretation of their findings hailing transracial placements as successful (in spite of the difficulties experienced by the vast majority of the study children around issues of racial identity) points to the assimilationist/intergrationsit philosophy of Gill and Jackson. Such "empirical dissonance" around actual findings and contradictory ideological conclusions is unhelpful and does much to obfuscate the issues.

Barbara Tizard (1977) has also carried out some work in the area of adoption. Her work is based on comparisons between three groups of children who originally spent some time in nursery care and then were either adopted, fostered long-term, or "restored" to their natural families. Tizard focused upon eight mixed-parentage children, all of whom were adopted after the age of two and followed up to the age of eight. Tizard found the placements to be extremely problematic. The families were said to be living in predominantly white areas and the children were experiencing immense difficulties in acknowledging their mixed racial origins and in forging links with black children.

Tizard also commented that the majority of the adoptive parents did not themselves have a positive feeling about the child's origins. She suggested that the transracial adopters in her study were trapped by an unconscious racial prejudice. Many of them saw "race" as akin to mental or physical "handicap", including one placement where the parent spoke of the child as having:

> ... *certain traits in his character which are definitely the traits of a coloured person. There's his lack of concentration. Also, he'll suddenly switch off if he thinks you're going to tell him off – he'll just go into his own little world. This is a thing that the coloured races do – one notices these little things.*

> (Tizard, 1977:181)

Such thinking where the perceived characteristics of an entire racial group come into play has been explored by Robert Miles in his study of migrant labour (Miles, 1982). The idea introduced by Miles is of relevance here, that is, since we are dealing with a situation where qualities of individuals are perceived to be representative of a wider collectivity (Miles, 1982:125). Thus if the individual is deemed to possess the criteria that designates membership of such collectivity, he or she is evaluated by the perceived qualities of the collectivity rather than the perceived qualities of the individual (Miles, 1982:126). Such negative labelling of an entire ethnic group points to the deeply embedded notions of racial superiority and inferiority.

Tizard (1977) found that by the age of eight, only four of the eight children had been told that they were of mixed parentage. This suggests that the concept of "race" could not have been discussed in those particular families. Despite her own evidence which suggests to the contrary, Tizard argued that only one of the eight children was a "cause for concern". This child, who had been adopted at the age of seven, continued to identify with a group of black children in his previous children's home. The fact that the child actually saw himself as black was seen as "cause for concern". This example also serves to illustrate the importance of going beyond a narrow, family-based focus on identity.

The ideological thrust of Tizard's work is revealed when she suggests that the problems involved in transracial placements are not surmountable by "same race" placements. Her commitment to the practice of finding permanent families for children in care leads her to suggest that social workers are unusually obsessed with blood ties. She argues that many social workers seek to return mixed-parentage children to unsatisfactory birth families or to black extended families that do not want the children, rather than place them in a white adoptive family where they would be wanted. Without having conducted any research into the rehabilitation of black children into their birth or extended families, and without the availability of any such evidence, it is not clear what leads Tizard to make such sweeping statements. Like the BAP studies, Tizard's study has been conceived in terms of one issue: whether or not transracial placements have been successful. This success has been measured by various methodological tools, including social work judgements, supposedly "objective" psychological tests, and portraits of the "experience" of the study families.

In 1989, Tizard and Phoenix asserted that there was no conclusive evidence to suggest that transracial placements were psychologically damaging for black children. Unlike Wilkinson and Koh (1985; 1988), they perceived identity in technical terms and failed to see a relationship between it and self-esteem. Indeed, Tizard and Phoenix asserted that:

> ... *it may be that young black people can have negative feelings about their racial identity, and yet have a positive self-concept.*
>
> (Tizard and Phoenix, 1989)

Thus they perceive racial identity and self-concept as two distinctly independent variables. Nick Banks, an African-American Clinical Psychologist, questions this "implausible" distinction. According to Banks, 'an integrated personality involves one having a stable concept of self as an individual as well as a group (Black) identity', whereby 'Black identity becomes an extension and indeed is part of the child's self-identity' (Banks, 1992:21). It is clear that the Eurocentric psychological perspectives require 'a significant perceptual shift to even begin to be relevant to considering the identity needs of black children and adolescents' (Banks, 1992).

14

In a study exploring the identities of a group of mixed-parentage children, Tizard and Phoenix (1993) pointed to the positive self-identity of these children. Whilst this in itself was a significant finding, it is important to discuss it in its context, that is, these children were not in the care system and came from stable home environments in multiracial areas that inculcated a healthy and positive identity. It is inappropriate to draw parallels between these children and those others whose identities are shaped by the negative experiences of the Eurocentric care system (Barn, 1994). Such a deductive approach to research serves to negate the issues and concerns of vulnerable black youngsters in the care system.

The 1989 Children Act which enshrined the notion of the importance of a child's racial, cultural, religious and linguistic background was a significant step (sec 22 (5) (c)). There is research evidence to show that local authorities are beginning to address issues of "race" and culture within this legal framework (Barn, 1993; Barn, Sinclair and Ferdinand, 1997; Waterhouse, 1997). However, it would seem that we in the UK may be following in the footsteps of the USA where it is now considered illegal, under the 1994 Multiethnic Placement Act, to attach importance to a child's racial and cultural background in making placement decisions about them (Bussiere, 1995). Moreover, the tide of neo-liberalist thinking in the once racially progressive state of California has resulted in the elimination of affirmative action in education and employment. This is likely to influence other states in the USA in reversing affirmative action policies.

In the UK, the backlash to the introduction of anti-racism teaching within social work education and training, and within social work policy and practice, indicates that we have not moved on a continuum of progress and change towards recognising structural inequalities. Moreover, the current revisitation to transracial placements, and the colour-blind emphasis of "love not colour" spearheaded by the former Junior Health Minister, Paul Boateng, is misguided and shortsighted. Whilst some black youngsters experience happy and stable homes, the social and psychological problems encountered by the majority of black youngsters in transracial family settings have been documented by research in both the UK and the US.

Black children in the public care system are subjected to a reality of isolation, alienation and marginalisation. Such children are particularly vulnerable in the absence of the black family and community. Cultural ignorance and various forms of racial prejudice and discrimination on the part of a system that purports to provide a caring environment further compound this. Developing strategies and techniques to work with these children to prevent/minimise negative experiences is absolutely crucial. Moreover, a framework where social processes and structures are targeted alongside individualised work is essential.

References

Banks, N. (1992) 'Techniques for direct identity work with black children'. In *Adoption and Fostering*, 16:3, pp 19–25.

Barn, R. (1993) *Black Children in the Public Care System*, London: Batsford/ BAAF.

Barn, R. (1994) *Black, White or Mixed-Race? Race and racism in the lives of young people of mixed-parentage*, Tizard, B. and Phoenix, A. (1993), London: Routledge, reviewed in *New Community*, 20:3.

Barnes, E. J. (1981) 'The black community as a source of positive self-concept for black children: a theoretical perspective'. In Jones, R. L. (ed) *Black Psychology*, 2nd edition, New York: Harper and Row.

Black and In Care (1984) *Black and In Care*, Conference Report, London: Blackrose Press.

Bussiere, A. (1995) *A Guide to the Multiethnic Placement Act of 1994*, Washington: American Bar Association.

Cheetham, J. (1981) *Social Work Services for Ethnic Minorities in Britain and the USA*, London: Department of Health and Social Security.

Chestang, L. (1972) 'The dilemma of biracial adoption'. In *Social Work*, 17, pp 100–115.

Divine, D. (1983) 'Defective, hypocritical and patronising research'. In *Caribbean Times*, 4 March.

Erikson, E. (1968) *Identity, Youth and Crisis*, London: Faber and Faber.

Gilroy, P. (1987) *There ain't no Black in the Union Jack*, London: Hutchinson.

Gilroy, P. (1993) *Small Acts*, London: Serpent's Tail.

Gill, O. and Jackson, B. (1983) *Adoption and Race*, London: Batsford/BAAF.

Koh, F. M. (1988) *Oriental Children in American Homes: How do they adjust?*, East West Press.

Herrnstein, R. J. and Murray, C. (1994) *The Bell Curve, Intelligence and Class Structure in American Life*, Simon and Schuster.

Maximé, J. (1993) 'The importance of racial identity for psychological well being of black children'. In *Association of Child Psychology and Psychiatry Newsletter*, 15:4, pp 173–179.

Multi-Ethnic Placement Act 1994, USA.

Miles, R. (1984) *Racism and Migrant Labour*, London: Routledge.

Milner, D. (1983) *Children and Race, Ten Years On*, London: Alan Sutton Publishing.

Raynor, L. (1970) *Adoption of Non-White Children: The Experiences of a British Adoption Project*, London: Allen and Unwin.

Rhodes, P. (1992) *Racial Matching in Fostering*, Aldershot: Avebury.

Rutter, M. (1985) 'Resilience in the face of adversity'. In *British Journal of Psychiatry*, vol. 147.

Small, J. (1984) 'The crisis in adoption'. In *International Journal of Psychiatry*, 30, Spring, pp 129–142.

Taylor, J. (1976) 'Psychological development among black children and youth: a re-examination'. In *American Journal of Orthopsychiatry*, 46, pp 4–19.

Tizard, B. (1977) *Adoption: A Second Chance*, London: Free Press.

Tizard, B. and Phoenix, A. (1989) 'Black identity and transracial adoption'. In *New Community*, 15:3, April.

Tizard, B. and Phoenix, A. (1993) *Black, White or Mixed-Race?*, London: Routledge.

Waterhouse, S. (1997) *The Organisation of Fostering Services: A study of the arrangements for delivery of fostering services in England*, London: NFCA.

Wilkinson, S. H. P. (1985) *Birth is More than Once: The inner world of adopted Korean children*, Detroit: Harlow Press.

2 Direct identity work

Nick Banks

Introduction

This chapter will consider techniques for direct therapeutic identity work with black children and young people. The distinction between "identity need", "identity difficulty" and "identity problem" will be briefly explored to allow workers to consider specific identity work. Furthermore, some prior self-exploration issues for black and white identity workers will be discussed and some cautions raised about conceptualising and carrying out identity work in isolation from other identified needs of the child. Techniques and strategies are explored in the context of case study material.

Assessing the need for direct identity work

One of the frequent criticisms that often arises is that child care professionals may often be too quick to suggest that black children need identity work. The reality that all children, regardless of ethnic background, need identity support is a fact often overlooked in planning the assessment and intervention needs of children looked after in substitute family care arrangements. Identity work is not a particular or sole need of black children. However, living in an often hostile and racist society means that the formation of a positive black identity is likely to need active, specific and targeted intervention and cannot simply be left to chance socialisation processes alone, as many of the socialising influences within white society will be antagonistic to the formation of a positive black identity.

It is perhaps necessary to define what is meant by a "positive black identity". Although some authors have expressed difficulty in understanding or defining this term (Tizard and Phoenix, 1989) my approach is one of attempting to operationalise or make explicit what might be the basic observable aspects of a "positive black identity". This is seen as being one where children have an unmistakable confidence and belief in self and own ethnic group worth, without being dismissive of other cultural or ethnic groups, and are able to accept and feel good about their own culture and "colour" without denigrating other groups. It is where the inner self is in harmony with one's physical appearance and ethnic group membership. Some may question whether this definition confounds the postulated separate categories of social and personal identity. I have dealt elsewhere with this argument as it affects black people (Banks, 1992) and those who wish to pursue this are referred to this previous article.

Having looked at how the term "positive black identity" can be defined, it is also necessary to consider when and how a not so positive black identity may show itself. It is useful to consider the continuum in Figure 1 to understand how the need for intervention may be conceived.

Figure 1
Indication of need for identity development intervention

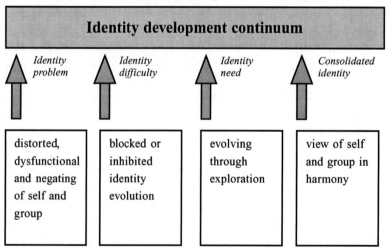

As has previously been suggested, all children have "identity needs". This may show itself in the context of "racial" or "ethnic" identity by a child asking the question, 'Where do I come from?' or asking, 'Why am I a different colour to Susan?' Here the young child, e.g. a three- or four-year-old, would be expressing a natural curiosity about their origins and observable differences between themselves and others. An "identity difficulty" may be shown when these questions are asked at an age, say nine or ten, suggesting that these fundamental issues about self, difference and belonging have not been satisfactorily addressed for the child by her or his carers. An "identity problem" on the other hand, may arise where an identity need has been ignored and this has, due to lack of appropriate exploration, become an "identity difficulty" which due to a continued lack of adequate exploration moves with the age, development and long-term unmet needs of the child to become an "identity problem". For instance, using the previous examples of the questions from children about origin and difference, many caregivers would not see a child of three to five years asking, 'Where do I come from?' as a difficulty, or 'Why am I a different colour to Susan?' as being an inappropriate question to ask in the young child's exploration of self and belonging. However, for those caregivers who would see these questions as difficult or uncomfortable to answer, or for those who give an answer wounding to the child's self-image, these topics may come to be perceived by the child as being taboo subjects such as asking about sexual matters on a crowded bus with a caregiver who is uncomfortable with how to handle such issues. The child may begin to believe that issues about self and difference should not/cannot be discussed openly and therefore suppress what should be a natural part of a child's exploration of self understanding.

The reader may wish to speculate whether and how white substitute carer families are prepared by the agencies that assess and select them to cope with these basic questions in a black child's "identity need" development. Caregivers who find "racial" or ethnic differences a difficult topic to discuss often protect themselves with assertions of "colour blindness" where they deny that there is any difference. Denying differences in colour and other physical ethnically related characteristics which are distinct and obvious to any three- or four-year-old may be the beginning of an intractable rift between a young child and caregiver that simmers at a young age and boils over into an unforeseen major issue in adolescence and early adulthood. When the realities of racist experience leave the black individual wounded and with a lack of resilience to cope with her or his obvious differences between black self and white society what were previously "identity difficulties" may emerge as "identity problems". As stated earlier it is when "identity needs" are unmet and drift into "identity difficulties" with questions that remain unanswered and issues unresolved that "identity problems" are likely to arise and come to the fore as needing specific intervention. Specific intervention is needed where a particular difficulty or problem arises and needs to be resolved before a child can be expected to move on successfully in their development without becoming "stuck".

It is necessary for the would be identity worker, whether black or white, to involve themselves in some self-assessment as to their motivational suitability for undertaking black identity work. Both black and white workers have a part to play in the support needs of black children's identity. To see this work as exclusively the role of black workers would, in effect, locate the responsibility for black children's development and care solely with black workers. Ultimately this line of thinking would allow white service providers to opt out of resource provision and delivery of services to meet the distinct cultural and physical needs of black children. There are a number of questions which should be answered before offering one's services as a potential identity worker.

Self-assessing personal suitability to offer direct identity work
The following separate lists for white and black workers are not seen as all inclusive lists of self-assessment questions. Rather, they offer the reader some guidance in considering their personal suitability for identity work.

Issues to be addressed by the white identity worker
- What is my motivation for engaging in such work? Do I know about my ethnic group history of colonial subjugation? Will I subtly perpetuate a colonial relationship?
- How do I feel when someone makes a racist remark?
- What actions have I taken to challenge racism amongst my own family, friends, community?
- What actions have I taken to challenge racism in the work place amongst my own colleagues ?
- How does racism impact upon me in my daily life?

- How do I feel when someone calls me a racist? How do I respond?
- What is my personal identification or relationship with the black communities?
- What do I like about being white?
- What do I feel about those who are physically, linguistically and culturally different?
- How does my image of black children differ from my image of black adults?
- What do I know about other people's cultures?
- What have I experienced of other people's cultures?
- How have I been involved in other people's cultures?
- How do I think of "blackness"?
- How have my experiences of being white shaped my views towards black people?
- How have I challenged and reversed negative images of black people? To what extent do these continue to exist? How do they show themselves?
- How would I react if my daughter, son, brother or sister wished to marry a black person? How would those around me react and how would I respond to these reactions?
- Will I further oppress black children by working through those difficulties with them which I have not resolved for myself?
- Do I have sufficient knowledge of child development as it relates to the development of children's understanding (language and cognitive development), racial awareness, social and emotional development?

Issues to be addressed by the black identity worker
- What is my experience, as a black person, of racism?
- How have I coped with this experience of racism? What strategies have I used?
- What are my earliest memories of being black and being different from white people? How did this make me feel? What did I do with these feelings?
- How do I feel about white people?
- Did I ever want to be white? How did this show itself? How did I resolve this?

- If I had negative thoughts about my blackness or black people, to what extent do these exist now? How have they been resolved?
- How has my experience of being black shaped my views towards black people? And towards white people?
- Will I further oppress black children by working through those difficulties with them which I have not personally resolved?
- Do I have a sufficient knowledge of child development as it relates to the development of children's understanding (language and cognitive development), racial awareness, social and emotional development?
- What do I believe is the place of the black person in white society?

The black and white workers, having considered the above suggested issues, will be better placed to assess what their particular training and supervision needs are. The responses to the questions should be thoroughly explored and following this it is very likely that further questions necessary for in-depth personal exploration will arise.

Case study examples of direct identity work

Justin

Justin was a five-year-old boy of African-Caribbean origin. One weekend he spontaneously said to his mother that when he 'turned white' he would also want her and his sister to 'turn white' at the same time. When his mother told him that they were a black family and none of them would ever turn white he became upset, crying and saying that he wanted to 'turn white'. His mother told him that he would always be black and he responded by saying, 'I'm not black, I'm brown'. His mother replied, 'You're not brown, you're black and you'll never be white'. Again, Justin cried further on hearing this.

It is suggested that Justin is showing an "identity difficulty" as previously discussed. The recommendations for identity work will be discussed as though the identity worker was not the parent. In some cases this will be appropriate and in other cases this will not be appropriate. The assessment of parental capacity to carry out direct identity work is beyond the scope of this chapter but should normally remain the preferred option as the positive nurturing that takes place within the black family tends to be of the highest quality and has a longer lasting effect compared to that of a professional agency's intervention which is usually based on white norms and values regardless of the ethnicity of the worker.

Several aspects of appropriate and sensitive work with children need to be acknowledged before the identity worker can begin work with Justin. Firstly, it is unlikely to be useful to pursue a line of questioning which starts with asking the child: 'Why do you want to be white?' This line of questioning may indicate several things about the questioner: 1) he or she is unable to relate to the experience of black children in a white racist society, and 2) he or she is searching for a single "trigger event" rather than seeing the wish to be white in a black child as part of a process over time. To some extent the reason why the child wishes to 'turn white' is obvious. Being white allows access to social privileges and removes the child from the position of being an object of ridicule, from abusive name calling and, in general, negative attention from white society. Furthermore, the use of questions starting with "why" may also attach to the child feelings of self-blame as questions starting with why may be associated with such questions as 'Why did you break the toy?' or 'Why did you hit your sister?', etc.

The searching for a single reason why a five-year-old black child wishes to be white, and attempting to extract this from the child by intense verbal questioning, as I have seen some workers attempt, is unlikely to be a productive path to follow. It may be experienced by the child as punitive. I suggest that the expressed wishes of the child are acknowledged and that a developmentally appropriate programme of intervention is planned. This programme should take into account that Justin is five years old and in denying that he is black and asserting that he is brown he is making a developmentally appropriate statement. Taking into account stages of cognitive development (Piaget and Inhelder, 1969) allows us to see that a five-year-old is likely to be only capable of thinking in very literal or concrete terms. A five-year-old is unlikely to see themselves as "black" unless they have had a history of preparation for this. The political meaning of the term is likely to be too complex and abstract for a five-year-old to understand. Thus, when Justin says he is not "black" but "brown", he is likely to be saying that in his literal understanding of the concept of colour he is lighter than the colour black would suggest. He may well be correct in his thinking and it would be oppressive for an identity worker to attempt to force the five-year-old to accept this possibly inaccurate description of themselves. A child seeing and accepting themselves as brown is, in my opinion, an acceptable view of self in terms of a child's cognitive understanding. Therefore, his assertion that he is brown is not cause for concern. The cause for concern is indicated by the wish to 'turn white' indicating at Justin's age, an "identity difficulty".

It would seem possible, and indeed likely, that issues of colour and difference have not been adequately explored with Justin at an earlier age and have therefore erupted at age five with Justin imagining an impossible bodily change. Rationalising or arguing with Justin, with attempts to coerce him into accepting his difference from white children, are unlikely to be successful identity support strategies, as they are punitive and not comforting or reassuring to the child. The lack of comfort and reassurance will not be likely to result in allowing the child to openly explore, eventually accept and actually internalise a view of self based upon positive self-discovery and acceptance.

Justin's "identity difficulty" is unlikely to be resolved by the exploration of issues of black history, food or culture. These are things that may be usefully explored at a later stage, but the exploration of "others" or things distant or abstract to the child is unlikely to be related to and understood as having meaning for or relevance about self to a five-year-old child. In short, explorations in black history, particularly if one uses material that is too complex for the child to engage with, are likely to be a "turn off" and have the opposite of the desired effect, i.e. the child may be further distanced from the locating of self within the black community.

A more effective starting point is likely to be one of examining and attempting to affect how a child feels about and sees him or herself. At this point we can only talk about Justin's "identity difficulty" in wishing to change his colour. What is it that Justin does not like about his colour? Note that this question has a very different emphasis than the question, 'why do you want to be white?' discussed earlier. However, although the identity worker may use this as an idea to drive the work they do with the child and areas of difficulty to specifically target, the actual asking of this question to a five-year-old is cautioned against and, in fact, any proposed intervention that has an over-reliance on language or verbal interaction is not recommended. A simpler and more useful starting point may be to ask the child to draw him/herself. A child's drawing of him/herself for the purposes of exploration should be carefully planned. Adequate blank paper and a range of coloured pencils and crayons should be available. However, this range should be restricted to no more than about six crayons, for example, black, dark brown, light brown, orange, green, and blue. There is sufficient here for the child to both realistically depict his or her skin colour and to avoid depicting it by choosing an unrepresentative crayon colour (this may suggest an "identity problem").

Justin chose a dark brown crayon and drew himself with blue shoes. The writer then asked Justin to say something about the picture which he (the author) could record. Justin said, 'This is me playing football'. The writer wrote beneath the picture what Justin had said and then added, 'Justin is a clever brown boy, who is good at playing football'. This was an attempt to raise the issue of colour and use the self descriptive skin colour label without an inappropriate face-to-face verbal confrontation. Here, the identity worker is simply reinforcing what the child has already drawn and made clear by his choice of crayons. By verbalising the "clever brown boy" one is attaching or associating aspects of positive connotation to difference and showing the child that this difference can be discussed or mentioned without emotional pressure being brought into play by the worker. Once the short story is read out no further discussion need take place. This initial session did not last more than ten minutes and was sufficient to ascertain how Justin saw himself, and to show Justin that colour and colour difference were not issues to be avoided and did not create tension with the identity worker when raised. The lessening of tension around exploration of issues of colour and colour difference allows the child in future sessions to raise his or her own agenda for exploration without apprehension.

The reader may at this point be wondering what the identity worker should do if the initial session does not go as smoothly as in the example above. Suppose the child draws a picture of him/herself but does not colour him/herself a shade of brown or black? In an initial session, which serves as an assessment session, where the child colours him/herself other than an ethnically applicable colour, the worker should avoid any action or discussion which may lead to confrontation or upset in the child. It is not possible at this early point to say whether this is an "identity problem" as we do not know the strength of resistance or do not have additional information about how the child is functioning in other areas related to their self concept and view of ethnic group membership.

Nargis

Nargis was a 14-year-old South Asian girl of mixed parentage, i.e. with a white English mother and Pakistani father. This case study has been especially selected to illustrate the considerations that should be taken into account where there is a "cluster of difficulties" in the child's life – not all related to ethnic identity – and where these difficulties have some bearing on additional work that needs to take place with the child.

Although named Nargis at birth, Nargis disliked her Muslim name and had adopted the name of Susan. Nargis had come into care at the age of eight due to complications in her mother's pregnancy with another child which had resulted in her mother's and the unborn child's death. The whereabouts of Nargis' father were unknown and his family had rejected her as a relative as her mother had not been married to her father. Nargis' maternal family had also rejected her due to the father being South Asian.

At the age of nine, Nargis had been placed with white English short-term foster carers who subsequently became her long-term foster carers. These foster carers lived in a mainly white working class area and had not received training in the additional demands that white foster carers were likely to encounter in attempting to meet the needs of a black child of mixed parentage. Nargis had adopted the name of Susan at about age ten as a means of avoiding the constant questioning by her peers as to why she had a "funny sounding" name. Her Muslim name drew immediate attention to her ethnic background and when this became known she was often called "Paki". Calling herself Susan allowed Nargis, to a limited degree, to escape the constant questioning about her background but the fact that she had a darker complexion from her white peers could not be avoided. To attempt to avoid the invasive probing of others she referred to her background as Italian.

In addition to identity difficulties, Nargis had unresolved issues around her mother's sudden death, what she saw as abandonment and rejection by her unknown (to her) father, maternal and paternal extended family. Moreover, the social services department was considering removing Nargis from her foster carers to place her with a South Asian family. Nargis was resisting this placement not because they were South Asian but due to the fact that they were elderly, inactive and ate hot spicy food to which she was not accustomed. Furthermore, she had developed an attachment to her foster carers who had offered her stability at a time of great change.

This case illustrates the appalling position in which some black children can find themselves when their needs are not sensitively identified and met at the outset. Nargis was treated more as a commodity to place and dump rather than having an assessment to find a foster family who would have been more responsive to her overall needs. It appeared at this point that her needs were quite complex and that those which would need to be prioritised would be those related to the loss of mother and, to a lesser extent, her sibling. Furthermore, the loss of and rejection by the extended family would need to be addressed before a further placement could be considered. The South Asian family that had been targeted for Nargis was, at a personal level, not suitable and to coerce her into "acceptance" would have been to further compound her bereavement and grieving through the loss of her present foster family with whom she had formed an attachment. It seemed that to move her would be once again treating her as a commodity rather than a person.

A family placement based on ethnic or cultural matching alone would be unlikely to happen with a white child. The question of why it should happen with a black child must be asked. Social services, having made several errors of judgement in allowing Nargis to drift in care unsupported, now needed to address the identified issues.

Before any future placement plans could be made for Nargis, bereavement counselling needed to be set in motion. Secondly, Nargis would need to be involved in the assessment and selection of a future suitable family and her views sought on what this constituted. The perceptions Nargis has of the rejection by her maternal and paternal extended families need to be therapeutically explored with Nargis. It may be that Nargis blames herself for all that has happened to her, and this self-blame is likely to block Nargis emotional and psychological development as a young woman.

As the child or adolescent does not operate in a social vacuum, the present foster carers should be involved with training to allow them to better consider and meet the needs of Nargis as a young black woman developing in a mainly white environment. As well as intervention with the substitute family, bereavement counselling, and involvement of Nargis in selecting an alternative ethnically matched family, there are issues around Nargis' perception of self. Furthermore, a sole focus on Nargis and her family is not appropriate as work needs to be done with the school to combat the racism Nargis experiences. The adoption of the name Susan is a means of defence that is easily understood. Thus, this was not an attempt or mechanism of denial but used as a means of escaping an oppressive position. It may be that Nargis is unlikely to become comfortable with her Muslim name until she becomes strong enough to deal with the persecution that the name attracts and gain some understanding of the effect it has upon her.

Direct work with Nargis would be possible in parallel with the grief and bereavement work. Some may wish to suggest life story work as a singular means to address Nargis' feelings of loss, rejection and ethnic identity difficulty. While this may sometimes be appropriate for some issues, I would not see it as appropriate for direct identity work in this specific case as this particular technique has a social matrix focus in its emphasis on looking at others and self in relation to others rather than an individual personal emphasis allowing Nargis to explore the way she feels about herself. Life story work, in practice, often becomes unfocussed and attempts to deal with all things at once without a critical appraisal of its limitations. Adolescents are particularly sensitive to how they perceive themselves to appear to others and I would attempt to tap into that sensitivity by allowing Nargis the exploration of her physical appearance to become more comfortable.

Mirror work could be one useful starting point. This type of work, as with any form of identity work, requires careful planning including appraising the terminology used and vocabulary expansion. Is the worker's vocabulary sensitive and appropriate for the description of an adolescent's physical appearance? Is it likely to facilitate self-acceptance and contentment or might it further arouse feelings of persecution through maintaining or creating discomfort around ethnically different physical characteristics, e.g. the shape of the nose, eyes and hair texture? Further, in mirror work with a child who has been sexually abused, the identity worker may have an additional issue and area of caution to consider if "flattery" of physical appearance, mistakenly perceived by the child or adolescent as the focus of mirror work, has been used in the abuse "grooming" process. Here, exploration of physical difference may bring back memories of the abusive experience. The identity worker is therefore advised to take this into account and further consider the vocabulary and effect.

The material needed for the technique of mirror work, as apparent by the name, is a mirror. The size of the mirror is not too important as long as all of the face and head can be seen and the subject and worker can get a view of the image. The worker should select a room for confidential work without interference by telephone, intrusion by others, or knocks on the door. The identity worker would then invite Nargis to describe how the identity worker looks. If a global description is given, the worker may need to say, 'Tell me what my face looks like to you'. The description may require further expansion of detail and if so the identity worker should invite this. The identity worker may then say, 'Now it's my turn to describe you'. An appropriate description for this type of work as it applied to Nargis would have been: I see a girl who has large, round brown eyes with long eyelashes. Your cheeks are raised and proud. Your skin is like that of an Indian princess and your hair is black and silky like the night. The reader must consider the impact of "self" in using these phrases. For example, it may be that white and black workers using these phrases may be received differently. A personal assessment of "self" in the context of direct work with the black child would need to take place.

The reader will see that as well as objective descriptive terms, the identity worker may bring in "imaginative association", e.g. "like an Indian princess" or "the night". This is an attempt to shift the negative associations that a child may have towards their characteristics and to make these positive associations. As was previously suggested the identity worker will need to avoid sexualised innuendoes.

The description of a black child's nose and lips will prove, in the writer's experience, to be difficult due to the lack of linguistically suitable terms in the English language. The error that can be made leading the child to withdraw is that related to the choice of an offending term, e.g. flat nose, thick lips, frizzy hair. This relates to the earlier expressed need to consider and plan beforehand the vocabulary that will be used. Rather than be drawn into unwanted and meaningless anatomically correct descriptions, the identity worker may need to consider the use of "imaginative association" so as to facilitate the open exploration of how a child or adolescent sees him/herself to be. In some cases the identity worker will need to go beyond the English language to obtain the appropriate vocabulary. For example, to capture the cultural significance and symbolism of the "Ghuta/Jurdha" (rather than top knot) or "distarr" (rather than turban) for Sikh people, the Punjabi words will need to be reinstated to move away from the negative, ridiculing associations that the phrase "handkerchief on head" will carry.

The aim of mirror work is to allow a mutual trust and reciprocity of exploration to take place about how each other looks. Although many different identity work techniques can be used by both black and white workers, in my experience the mirror work technique works best, i.e. with the greatest self-exploratory effect, with workers who have the same skin tone as the child or adolescent. The facilitating effect appears to be one of allowing the child to explore self through the acceptance others of similar background have of themselves. Although this is a valuable added dimension for the identity worker and client who are of similar ethnic background, it should not inhibit those of a dissimilar background from attempting mirror work.

It has been suggested that it may be unproductive to focus on issues related to history and food at inappropriate times in the development of the child. Another common action is to attempt to teach the young child about racism. This clearly has its place in identity work although it can be overdone through a well meaning sense of protection in preparation for later experience. The destructive element may be that of blaming or labelling all white people as racists and not appropriately exploring the child's experience of racism. A picture that is painted of all white people as doing potential damage to the child may have the effect of disabling the child in making his or her way in the white world. The point that is being made is that the concept of racism is an abstract one that young children will not readily grasp. The information that is picked up will only be partially understood and may have the unintended effect of the child withdrawing from contact with white people. Claiming that all white people are racists presents a frightening horror story that may have some far reaching effects in the child's social and emotional development.

Conclusion
The process of positive identity formation in the black child is not something that can happen overnight. It is often after a long struggle and dedicated attempts that it is reached. As with any attempt at intervention, suitable training may need to take place before a worker can carry out identity work. Although there are ways of doing direct work which I would see as ineffective, inappropriate or harmful, there is no single right way. In any attempt at direct work, appropriate prior planning must take place and adequate time for rapport building and the establishment of trust should be allowed. In attempting to explore and meet the needs of the child, the identity worker may need to be prepared to encounter unforeseen issues. These may require exploration of how best to investigate or pursue resolution through the use of skilled supervision arrangements which help with the interpretation of issues that arise in order for further techniques to be considered. Direct identity work should not take place without proper training and supervision. Black children are too precious to be used simply as a learning facility for the development of workers' skills.

References

Banks, N. (1992) 'Techniques for direct identity work with black children'. In *Adoption and Fostering*, 16:3, pp 19–25.

Piaget, J. and Inhelder, B. (1969) *The Psychology of the Child*, London: Routledge and Kegan Paul.

Tizard, B. and Phoenix, A. (April 1989) 'Black Identity and Transracial Adoption'. In *New Community*, 15:3.

3 Identity project on 'myself' with pre-schoolers at a day nursery

Alice Sawyerr

Introduction

Providing assessments and therapeutic sessions to referred children and their families on site at a local authority nursery (which offers services to paying and non-paying parents/carers) has been challenging, enjoyable and a good learning process. Over the past five years I have struggled to find imaginative, creative, flexible and pragmatic ways of engaging and working with adults and children inside and outside of the nursery system. The following is a narrative account of this experience which could provide pointers for professionals working with children in different settings.

Location

The nursery is now one of six day nurseries run by the education department of the local council. It is a large building which was set up as a day nursery during the second world war. It offers the equivalent of 45 full-time places and has the equivalent of nine full-time qualified NNEB and Nursery Nursing B Tec. nursery officers. It is located in a multicultural and multiracial community, where black and white families have lived and intermarried for several decades. Many of their children have attended the nursery and now so are their grandchildren. There are also British born children from newly arrived immigrant families from Asia, North Africa and Eastern European countries attending the nursery whose parents speak little or no English.

The nursery is staffed by African/African Caribbean, White, Middle Eastern and Asian nursery officers (which to some extent reflects some of the racial and cultural backgrounds of the children at the nursery).

A key worker system operates within the nursery. The key worker's role is to ensure that the children and their parents/carers are offered stability and continuity. The key worker monitors each child's development and learning and sets a series of personal goals for him/her. Parents are expected to work closely with their child's key worker, and together share information which will assist the child to develop to his/her full potential. Each child has a Care and Educational Plan after three months of settling in; this is reviewed every six months or more often as appropriate. Parents/carers and children are encouraged to contribute to these plans.

The nursery's philosophy is to provide a stimulating and safe environment for all the children. It has a structured programme of activities, each designed to allow the children to learn through fun, imagination and thoughtful guidance.

Access to nursery placement
Access to the day nursery is by three methods:
- A referral by the social services department for children who come under children "in need" of a place.
- Via the Early Years Development Plan for three- and four-year-olds whose parents want places.
- Privately on a "first come first served" basis.

Early Years Curriculum
The Early Years Curriculum programmes are broad, balanced and differentiated to meet the age and development of each child. Programmes are displayed in the nursery and are planned around the six topics of the Desirable Learning Outcomes and the Local Council's Curriculum for the Under-fives, namely: mathematics, language and literacy, personal and social development, knowledge and understanding of the world, physical development and creative development.

The nursery celebrates various world and religious events as part of extending the children's knowledge and understanding of the world. Some of the events which are celebrated include Eid, Diwali, Chinese New Year, Easter, Christmas, St Patrick's Day and many others. These involve story reading, entertainment, displays, meals and parties in which the parents/carers are asked to participate, as well as to share their knowledge and experiences with the staff. The nursery also provides services for children with special needs as far as possible.

Identified need for the project

The need for the development of the Identity Project centring on *Myself* as a theme grew from an awareness within the staff team of the pre-school age group (three–five-year-olds) that some children were either struggling with or were unaware of their racial and cultural backgrounds, e.g. some children of "mixed-race" parentage were referring to themselves as white and some black children were referring to themselves as "quarter caste" at nursery because their white grandmothers had insisted at home that they were "quarter caste". They in turn were asking their Asian and lighter complexioned black peers at nursery whether they were also "quarter caste".

- There were ambivalent feelings amongst some of the parents and staff about when and how to introduce the concept of self, "race", culture and identity to the children.
- There were apparent difficulties for minority ethnic and, in particular, black and mixed parentage children in identifying with their skin colour, heritage and cultural issues.
- Some children were receiving mixed messages from their parents/ grandparents/carers and from some nursery staff about their racial and cultural identity.
- Others were receiving no input from their parents/carers or staff about their racial and cultural identity.

Attempts made by nursery staff to address the issues

The availability and easy access to multicultural activities, group outings, celebrations of world and religious events, reading materials and other resources in the nursery, did not appear to have made any substantial difference to the level of understanding needed by the children to develop their sense of self. For the most part, some white and some black staff members had assumed that, if the children were regularly exposed to relevant activities, resources and group discussions from workers of diverse ethnicities and cultures, the children would inevitably develop an awareness of their identity and concepts of self.

As the children's lack of awareness and seeming confusion about their identity increased, it became clear to one of the black key workers in the pre-school group that urgent action needed to be taken to address these issues and that outside specialist help was necessary.

Previous attempts made to address the issues

It is worth noting that, three years earlier, I had identified some of these issues and had offered joint consultation sessions with a white colleague to the entire nursery staff team and management; I am black African. However, our efforts had been met with a lot of resistance. The consultation sessions were cancelled on the scheduled days due to reported staff unavailability. In the event the consultation sessions had to end even though there had been approval and apparent commitment from senior management.

As my work with individual children and their families at the nursery continued (90 per cent of which were referrals from the pre-school group), I began to encourage and engage with the key workers in joint sessions with the children on site as well as off site. These involved observations of the parent–child sessions, family sessions (from behind the one way screen with the families' consent), and in debriefing sessions. Over time the key workers began to develop a keen interest in the sessions especially when they began to observe marked positive changes in the children's behaviour at nursery.

Request for specialist help

Following the identification of the issues by a key worker from the pre-school group and the need for specialist help being recognised and agreed to from within the nursery system, a direct referral was made to myself by the concerned black key worker, with support from the white manager for consultation.

The rationale for my choice of intervention

My assessment was that the identified children were not showing signs of "pathology" and therefore did not require individual therapy. They were, in my view, based on normal development for ages three to five years, showing curiosity about identity and self-concepts, a normal part of socio-emotional development. Cognitively, they were demonstrating the beginnings of their acquisition of the ability to think, to notice small details and accurately observe discrepancies, to remember and report things that had happened to them, and to make interesting associations. Part of children's normal language development involves asking "why" "when" and "how" questions of the significant adults in their lives, requiring simple answers and recounting the content of stories even though they may misinterpret facts or confuse details.

In my professional view, it was the nursery staff and some of the parents/carers who were feeling stuck and who needed support in understanding the issues and finding helpful ways of addressing them. Much clarity and collaborative work between the adults in the system were needed. Secondly, since these were normal stages that all children have to go through, it was imperative that both white and black children and their parents/carers be involved in the project.

Following a detailed referral meeting with the three black key workers and their white manager and deputy manager, a schedule was developed for weekly two-hour consultation sessions. There was an agreement and commitment from the staff and management that:

- the three key workers from the pre-school group and management staff would attend and actively participate in the weekly two-hour sessions;
- an identity project centring on the theme *Myself* would be developed to address the issues affecting the children's sense of self; and
- it was imperative to involve and engage all the parents/carers, children and staff in the pre-school group in the project activities.

Aims and objectives
The main aims of the project were:
- to help the children develop a strong image of themselves;
- to help the children in the pre-school group to look at themselves (including physical features) with their key workers and families and to feel more positive about themselves and their families;
- to help the children know and feel comfortable with their racial and cultural identity;

- to encourage awareness amongst the children about different racial and cultural backgrounds;
- to prepare the children for the challenges of the school environment, to feel confident and proud of themselves, their racial and cultural identities, and those of their families; and
- to raise awareness amongst the staff and parents within the whole nursery of the importance of the children's identity and development of pride and clarity in the children's sense of self.

The consultation process

Stage 1

This involved four weeks of training workshops for the three key workers and two managers, before the start of the project, in which the following areas were explored:

- The meaning of "race", culture, religion, and spirituality for each nursery officer.
- Which communities were considered to be minority ethnic communities in Britain today.
- The meaning of the term black: who is considered to be black? Where do black people come from? Are they a homogeneous group or not? And if not, why not?
- The knowledge, guiding principles, values, beliefs, and assumptions that nursery officers bring with them in their negotiations with parents/carers.
- The needs, cultural beliefs, values, knowledge and child-rearing experiences and practices that parents/carers bring with them in their negotiations with nursery officers.
- The expectations of parents/carers of the nursery officers in relation to their children.
- The negotiation process, the knowledge, skills, attitude and experience needed to work cross-culturally and interculturally, i.e. how to join in with and engage families from diverse racial and cultural backgrounds in the identity project centring on *Myself.*

Some exercises were given in the workshops to aid some of the understanding needed to accomplish the task.

Stage 2

This involved a workshop in which the key concepts and materials to be used in the project were introduced:

- Copies of *Black Like Me, Workbook One* by Dr. Jocelyn Maximé were distributed to each worker. Some time was spent on adapting, redefining and elaborating on the activities on self and identity in the book to meet the specific needs of the children in the pre-school group, given their age, multicultural and multiracial backgrounds e.g. gathering information about grandparents, religion, dress worn on special occasions, languages spoken at home, favourite foods, foods eaten at home, etc.

- In *Black Like Me, Workbook One*, Dr. Maximé prescribes the child's identity as African. However, in this project a variety of identity categories were listed and the parents/carers were asked to choose a category with their child that best described the child's identity. For parents/carers who did not see their child as exclusively black, Asian or white, etc. they were asked to choose from an additional category which listed a series of terms describing mixed parentage identities, the terminology that they and their child felt was appropriate. They were also asked to indicate the identity of each parent.

- Plain exercise books, plastic mirrors, skin tone crayons, skin tone papers, colour pencils for eyes and hair, envelopes containing the suggestions/guidelines for 19 activities and a plastic case for storing the above materials were prepared for each parent/carer and their child.

Stage 3

In this stage, the key nursery officers used the consultation session to plan a step-by-step programme on how the activities would be implemented with the children at nursery and with the parents/carers at home. The starting and finishing dates for the project were decided and each worker was given the task of drafting a letter to parents/carers about the project, indicating the purpose and duration of the project, in preparation for the next consultation session.

Stage 4

Ideas from each staff member's draft letter to parents/carers about the project were incorporated into one letter, which was hand delivered to the parents/carers by the respective key workers on the Friday before the project was launched (the following Monday).

It was agreed that the weekly two-hour consultation sessions would continue throughout the life of the project: I would provide support and guidance to individual key workers as needed and would also be available at short notice to the parents/carers for support, clarification, and help in dealing with sensitive issues and questions that may come up in the work with their children at home.

Joint activities with parents/carers, children and key workers

The identity activities with the key workers, parents/carers and children were implemented over a six-week period. All ten children (four girls and six boys) and their parents/carers agreed to participate in the project; no parent/carer from the pre-school group refused to participate with their child.

The plastic cases containing the materials and identity activities were given to the parents/carers each day with verbal explanations from the respective key worker prior to its completion at home with the child.

Some parents asked to spend some time at the nursery with their child and the key worker to complete each activity because of language and literacy difficulties. Others requested individual sessions with me before commencing the activities with their child, because of sensitive emotional issues that they felt they needed to work through for themselves e.g. being adopted and not knowing about their own biological parents and therefore feeling insecure about their own identity. For others still it was the realisation that they needed to deal with their feelings of anger and hurt in relation to their absent partners, in order to help their child make sense of who they were and who their parents and family members were.

Methodology

The two part-time key workers had responsibility for three children each; the full-time key worker had responsibility for four.

The role of the key worker

Before the actual work started with the children, each key worker met with the parents/carers of their key children to:

- Discuss the letter they had received about the project, introduce me and explain my role as consultant to the project as well as being an experienced and trained Family and Systemic Psychotherapist who would be available at short notice on request for support and/or clarification and help in dealing with sensitive issues that may come up in their work with their children at home.
- Discuss any immediate practical difficulties that the parents/carers felt may arise which would affect the completion of the activities with their child at home.
- Go through the suggested guidelines and the list of 19 activities that would be used in the children's books.
- Answer questions and address issues that they may have about the 19 activities to be completed.
- Explain how the work would be done, what resources would be used, and to ask them whether or not they wanted to be involved in the project.

The process

The project was carried out using the prepared materials/resources. Each child was allocated their own resources and the process is described below.

- The key workers pasted the suggestions/guidelines on to the first page of each child's book.
- The parents/carers with their child chose a photograph of their child and pasted it on the outer cover of the book at home.
- Each activity was pasted onto a new page in the book by the key workers in sequence, one at a time, once the previous activity had been completed by the parents/carers and children.
- The key workers were responsible for sending the books home with the pasted activity sheet in them each day. The parents/carers were responsible for completing the activities at home each day with their child, signing the page, and for ensuring that the books were taken back to the nursery every morning.

- The key workers met with their respective parents/carers and key child each morning for feedback on the activity completed, as well as at the end of each day to explain how the newly pasted activity was to be completed.
- The first two activities were completed by the parents/carers and their children either at home or, with special arrangement, at the nursery.
- Three of the activities which covered facial features, skin colour, and hair were completed at the nursery with the key workers, as negotiated with the parents/carers during their initial planning meeting. The children were given mirrors and books specifically about "self" to look through. They were given time to discuss the facial features of the characters in the books which then led on to them looking at their own facial features and issues about themselves. The colour of their skin, eyes, hair texture, etc. were talked about. The children worked in pairs or individually with their key nursery worker. The sessions took place either in the group room or in a separate room. The time spent with each child varied from 15–30 minutes depending on how much work the child was able do at one time.
- The sessions which took place in the nursery with the parents/carers, their children and the key workers, were led by the parents/carers. The key workers' role was that of support and of giving guidance to the parents/carers when necessary, and not actually doing the activities with the children.

Each parent/carer was given an evaluation form to fill in at home on completion of all of the activities with their child. These were returned promptly.

Presentation of achievement certificates
With some of the children starting school at their fifth birthday, a party and presentation ceremony were organised at the nursery for all the children and parents/carers to mark their achievement. Each child was presented with a personalised colourful certificate for completing all the activities on the identity project. Pictures were taken of each child receiving their certificate from the staff. The parents/carers were called up alongside their child, congratulated for completing all the activities

Activity 19 was completed by the parents/carers and children with ethnic background as follows:

Sex of child	Ethnic Origin of child	Religion of child	Mothers's E.O. and religion	Father's E.O. and religion
Female	Mixed-parentage	Protestant	Mixed Caribb/White parentage (Protestant)	African Caribbean (Protestant)
Male	Mixed-parentage	Protestant	White Finnish (Protestant)	White Polish (Jewish)
Female	African-Caribbean	Catholic	African-Caribbean	African-Caribbean
Male	Pakistani	Muslim	Pakistani (Muslim)	Pakistani (Muslim)
Male	White	Catholic	White English (Catholic)	White Irish (Catholic)
Male	Mixed-parentage	Protestant	White English (Protestant)	African-Caribbean (Protestant)
Female	Mixed-parentage	Protestant	White Swedish (Protestant)	African-Nigerian (Protestant)
Female	African-Moroccan	Muslim	African-Moroccan (Muslim)	African-Moroccan (Muslim)
Male	African-Sudanese	Muslim	African-Sudanese (Muslim)	African-Sudanese (Muslim)
Male	Mixed-parentage	Catholic	Mixed-Parentage Brazilian (Catholic)	White Portuguese (Catholic)

with their child, and photographed with their child.

The certificate presentation ceremony was also video-taped. The ceremony ended with the key workers, management staff and the consultant joining in with the children and their parents/carers for an enjoyable Easter party celebration.

Stage 5
This involved a major review and evaluation of the entire project. The key workers, management staff and I met for half a day with our written assessments on the following areas of the project:
- The children's completed activity workbooks.
- The parents/carers' evaluation forms.
- The key workers', managers' and the consultant's evaluation forms.
- Feedback from the parents/carers and children on the certificate presentation day and ceremony.

A discussion on the processes involved, lessons learnt and possible ways forward for future projects were carefully explored and noted.

A major presentation of the project was made to senior managers from the local authority's education department, social services and the NHS Trust. All the children's completed activity workbooks, resource materials, completed evaluation forms, photographs and certificates were on display. They were also shown the video-tape of the certificate presentation ceremony.

Evaluation and recommendation
The overall assessment was that the project had been successful in meeting the outlined aims and objectives: The following areas were highlighted:
- Both written and verbal feedback from the parents/carers were very positive. All the parents/carers reported that the activities and processes involved had helped them and their children to address key issues relating to who they were in a formalised way which they had previously been unable to deal with on their own.
- For some of the parents, issues around absent fathers which had been difficult for them to talk about with their children were addressed through the activities with much sensitivity and professional support.
- All the parents/carers requested more interactive activities ("homework") with the nursery staff for their children. They reported that the

children were attentive and enjoyed completing the activities with them. It was meaningful and quality time was spent.

- There were also noticeable changes in the children's drawings of themselves and others at nursery e.g. particular attention being paid to skin tones, hair and eye colours and facial features in all their drawings subsequent to the project.
- The white children no longer left their drawings of themselves on white sheets of paper blank. They searched for the appropriate skin tone crayons for shading in their skin tone even though they were referred to by adults as "white".
- Similarly, the black, Asian and mixed parentage children shaded in drawings of themselves with the appropriate skin tones but not black even though some of were referred to as "black" by adults.
- All ten children were more able to describe themselves, their identity i.e. "race", culture, colour of their skin, nationality, language spoken at home, religion, clothes worn on special occasions and festivals where applicable, without any hesitation and with pride.
- They were also able, in group settings, to talk about observable similarities and differences in their skin tones, facial features, hair colours and textures in positive ways.
- The children took pride and great care in the handling of their Identity Activity Workbooks. There were no torn pages or marks in the books even though most of the books travelled daily between their homes and the nursery.
- The key workers and management staff acknowledged the value and importance of working jointly with parents/carers in addressing identity issues and concepts of self with pre-school age children.
- The identity project provided the nursery officers and the consultant with valuable opportunities to learn firsthand from the parents and the children about their cultures, histories, values and beliefs. Most of the parents were very creative in the work that they did with their children. The process had the effect of bringing the parents/carers and professionals closer together to work in equal partnership.
- Both parents/carers and staff were unanimous in their recommendation that the identity project should become a formalised and integral part of the pre-school group curriculum at the nursery.

This recommendation has been accepted and it is now an integral part of the pre-school curriculum. Plans are underway for its implementation in the five other local authority nurseries.

References

Maximé, J. (1994) *Black Like Me – Workbook One: Black Identity*, Emani Publications.

Maximé, J. (1994) *Black Like Me – Workbook Three: Mixed-Parentage*, Emani Publications.

4 Direct work with black children with a white parent

Beverley Prevatt Goldstein

Introduction

This chapter focuses on black children with a white parent, a group commonly referred to as "mixed race", "mixed parentage", or "dual heritage". Demographic trends suggest an increase in the number of children from this particular background (Owen, 1996). Barn (1999) shows that the most common family arrangement for mixed-parentage children under the age of 16 was to be living with a white mother in a couple. However, for the black- (African/African Caribbean) white mixed-parentage children, it was found that almost as many children lived with a lone white mother (53.2 per cent and 45.5 per cent respectively, see Phoenix and Owen, 1996). Moreover, research evidence shows that these children are significantly represented in the "looked after system" (Bebbington and Miles, 1989; Rowe *et al*, 1989; Barn, 1993; Barn, Sinclair and Ferdinand, 1997).

This chapter suggests ways of working with this group drawing both from social work and black perspectives. These suggestions are not prescriptive; rather they are offered as working guidelines to those parents/carers/professional workers working with black children with a white parent, guidelines which can be adapted and developed to meet the needs of the individual child and his or her situation.

This chapter, in highlighting the direct work that is specific to black children with a white parent, is rightly located in direct work with the wider group of black children. There is a great commonality of experience and the groups are so intertwined that much of the research and personal histories do not distinguish between them. But this should not obscure specificity of experience. The practice, advocated in this chapter, is that of recognising, valuing and responding appropriately to difference, and acknowledging the reality of common experiences, the benefits of solidarity and the dangers of divisiveness. This chapter, therefore, seeks to reinforce this good practice. "Black" is used throughout in its widest political sense with an awareness both of the current challenges to this (as reflected in Modood, 1988; Miles, 1994) and the rebuttals (Brah, 1992; Camper, 1994).

One definition of direct work is *a one-to-one relationship with a child developed to an intense level for the purpose of facilitating the child's greater sense of himself and his/her greater communication with significant others* (Dutton, 1995). Direct work therefore usually includes a focus on the child's self-concept and self-esteem and this will be considered in the first section of the chapter. Direct work is deemed to be best undertaken in the context of safety and when there is a "holding network" (Dutton, 1995). This security is necessary for children to let go of their survival strategies and consider alternatives ways of being and relating. Direct work around security will be considered in the second section of the chapter. Direct work with a child is primarily the province of parents and carers. The suggestions in these two sections are, therefore, directed to parents and carers of black children with a white parent and the professionals in health, education, social and community work who may support them. There is an additional context of direct work, when a child's behaviour is deemed to be signifying a deficit in their sense of self and relationship with others (self-harm, depression, aggressive behaviour) or when they have experienced circumstances which parents and professionals deem to impact negatively on their sense of self (abuse, separation and loss). Here social workers, therapists and other professionals become more clearly involved in direct work and the guidelines in the third section address their intervention. The guidelines recommended in each of these three sections will consider engaging at the following levels:

- the parent/carer/professional (direct worker) working on their own attitudes and assumptions;
- the direct worker gently and continuously providing the environment and support that enables the child to achieve the most positive outcomes; and
- the direct worker engaging with the child to directly address internalised and/or externalised negative feelings, while continuing to provide an appropriate environment and support.

In the fourth and final section there will be some consideration of the attributes most helpful in the worker (parent/carer/professional) undertaking direct work with black children with a white parent.

Direct work around self-concept and self-esteem

Social work with children is underpinned by normative assumptions about parenting and healthy development (Burman, 1994). White Eurocentric notions have been challenged from a black perspective leading to fiercely contested debates about the needs of black children and their appropriate parenting (ABSWAP, 1983; Maximé, 1986). Direct work with black children with a white parent falls into this contested area and care needs to be taken to be explicit about our underpinning frameworks. The black child with a white parent is the child of two people who have been constructed as "racial" opposites by much of present society. The child therefore has to develop a "racial" self-concept which manages this duality (in combination with a range of interlocking self-concepts – age, gender, sexuality, religion, ethnicity and so on). This is further complicated by the racism which rates black and white people differently and which pathologises the union of black and white (Paulse, 1994; Prevatt Goldstein, 1999). The development of self-concept and self-esteem will therefore require particular strategies but should not be pathologised (Owusu-Bempah, 1994; Prevatt Goldstein, 1997).

I would suggest that the desired outcome for a black child with a white parent is *that a child feels positive about themselves as a black child with a white parent and feels part of a group that contributes, survives, challenges.* The significance of the naming of black is partly to do with the likelihood of society's ascription (Small, 1986) but equally to do with the value that can be placed on a black identity and black solidarity (Younge, 1994; Prevatt Goldstein, 1999). The choosing to identify as black can signify a political identification with the oppressed and a rejection of the racism that encourages "passing" for white (Green, 1994). However, this does not necessarily mean a denial of white parentage:

> *I identify as Black but I am not ashamed of my non-black ancestry. I should be allowed to be who I am and so should everyone else. Just let's do it with enough awareness to know where we are really located.*
>
> (Camper, 1994, p. xxiv)

Guidelines for developing self-concept

Direct work with black children with a white parent around self-concept and self-esteem needs to be based on the knowledge that a healthy, positive self-concept is both possible and commonplace (Wilson, 1987; Tizard and Phoenix, 1993; EYTARN, 1995). It then needs to incorporate a valuing of both black and white people, cultures and ways of being. The parent/carer/worker may first need to confront their own racism (Mama, 1995) which may lead them to prefer white to black, to be wary of acknowledging the reality of racism, and wary of the need to positively and proactively value black people. Those situated in a black radical discourse (Mama, 1995) need to be sufficiently secure in this discourse to accept white as positive. All must avoid homogenising and subscribing to stereotypical notions of black and white and strive to accept and demonstrate to the children they are working with diversity within and similarities between each of these socially constructed groupings.

Secondly, the parent/carer/worker needs to demonstrate by the world with which they surround the child e.g. language, toys, books, pictures, television, schools, neighbourhoods, peers, supporting adults, that black people and white people are valued. This has to recognise the external reality that white is often preferred to black and a child will absorb this unless the direct worker provides a context where black is positively and pro-actively valued and racism named, in a way appropriate to the child's age, understanding and support systems. While it is also essential that a child values their white parentage, this is usually facilitated by the white media and white dominated society in Britain. However, direct work with black children with a white parent needs to encourage children to value the breadth of their diversity. Derman-Sparks (1980) suggests that highlighting those white people who have worked for peace and justice may be a positive way of valuing white parentage while acknowledging inequality. At this stage the direct worker is providing the building blocks for a child to develop a self-concept which can incorporate and value black and white in the context of racism. The worker can then respond in the direction and at the pace set by the child.

The third level is necessary to the extent that a child has internalised a negative evaluation of black (a negative evaluation of white is less likely in this society) or rejects duality and complexity. This requires a

more active stance on the part of the direct worker, more targeted
conversations and focused resources. But this still needs to be at a pace
appropriate to the developmental age of the child and with an
understanding that moving between self-concepts is common (Jayaweera,
1993; Woolett *et al*, 1994; Mama, 1995) and manageable:

> *i am fusion*
> *all that stuff iz yor confusion*
> *multi-faceted not fragmented*
> *i kover the spektrum*
> (McNeilly, 1994, p. 219)

Direct work around self-concept and self-esteem also needs to be based
on a recognition that being black with a white parent is normal. Again,
action at the first level requires the direct worker to fully accept this
themselves, so that they can convey this to the child. Pathologisation of
black and white unions arising from racism (Prevatt Goldstein, 1999)
may hinder this acceptance by white workers. Black workers may also
react negatively to these unions viewing them as demonstrating internalised racism and a devaluing of black relationships by black people
(Modood, 1997) though the comparatively higher proportion of black/
white relationships among black communities compared to white communities suggests that this view is perhaps not widely nor strongly held
(Owen, 1996). Direct workers from black communities where a substantial proportion of the children have a white parent e.g. African-
Caribbean, may, regardless of their political views, find it easier to
recognise the normality of black children with a white parent.

Action at the second level requires that the child is surrounded by a
world which reinforces this normality e.g. language, toys, books,
pictures, play mates, other adults, neighbourhoods, schools, yet avoids a
racist distancing or feelings of superiority towards black children with
two black parents (or who are more visibly black). As the child is still
likely to be part of the wider world with its norm that "white is best" and
in the majority of cases have a principal carer (mother) who is white
(Owen, 1996), action is unlikely to be needed to validate white as normal.
An awareness of well known black people with a white parent e.g. Bob
Marley or Mary Seacole, who did not distance themselves from black

communities, may be shared via stories, music, drawing, worksheets to reinforce this normality.

At the third stage, where the child may have internalised ideas of abnormality, there needs to be a more explicit emphasis on black and black/white being normal, though eschewing panic, pathologisation or moving beyond the child's pace. It remains essential to reinforce diverse normalities so that the child does not consider there is one way of being black with a white parent or that any other parenting configuration is less "normal".

Black children with a white parent often experience society's ambivalence. They may be perceived as nearly white, not really black, black, in-between, confused, able to choose, with the ground shifting depending on the age, sexual maturity, skin colour of the young person as well as the agendas of the other people involved. A black person with a white parent is frequently challenged on their identity:

> *People used to ask me. That made me realise that it isn't normal, or they think it isn't normal for someone to have a black dad and a white mum. That made me different. I never used to like it.*
>
> (Tizard and Phoenix, 1993, p. 91)

> *Despite my self-identification as Black, people would ask me what I was mixed with.*
>
> (Paulse, 1994, p. 47)

This experience of inconsistency and powerlessness is an additional dynamic in working with black children with a white parent. The direct worker needs to support the child in managing ambivalence and change; be alongside the child if he or she wishes to explore different ways of seeing and of naming themselves; help the child, through naming racism, struggle and provide solidarity in ways appropriate to the child's age, understanding and support systems; and recognise the context and consequences of different self-concepts.

Guidelines for developing self-esteem
Studies have shown (Gill and Jackson, 1983; Jackson *et al*, 1997) that children can have a high self-esteem that ignores aspects of their reality.

This may be an adequate coping strategy for some children, for some time, but direct work usually seeks to facilitate developments that can carefully integrate reality. This requires care as the child will occasionally find this integration of two "opposites" or the acceptance of black identification difficult. Tizard and Phoenix's research showed that of the 51 per cent of children who had wished to be another colour, 70 per cent had wished to be white, and 20 per cent had wished to be just one colour, either black or white (1993, p. 54). Self-esteem based on reality requires action at all three levels. The worker must themselves consider being black with a white parent as positive, eschewing notions of pathology, inevitable identity conflict, and so on (Owusu-Bempah, 1994). They must build in careful, understated and continuous work to promote self-esteem based on this reality in the following ways, for example, by:

- surrounding the child with significant others who are positive about this aspect of the child;
- providing positive role models who mirror this aspect of the child;
- highlighting the positives of this aspect to the child; and
- providing opportunities for a general feeling of well-being and achievement that encompasses more than being black with a white parent.

If the child feels negative about this aspect of themselves, the direct worker needs to consider doing the above more actively and directly. However, it is essential that self-esteem based on being black with a white parent does not lead, in a racist society, to distancing and devaluing other black people (with two black parents or darker skins) or to being developed in isolation. All aspects of the child including gender, age, sexuality, (dis)ability, and ethnicity need to be valued in ways that enable the child to feel comfortable with all of themselves. The direct worker needs to recognise that each area is important and may require a discrete focus at any or all of the three levels outlined in the introduction; that different areas will have priority for different children at different times and that each area will impact on the other. This work around self-concept and self-esteem is greatly facilitated by increasing the security felt by the child. To do this "identity" work without tackling the abuse the child may be experiencing is equivalent to offering a child therapy around sexual abuse while allowing the sexual abuse to continue.

Direct work around security

It is essential that the direct worker is aware of the likely external world of the black child with a white parent and makes every effort to make it a safe place. Racism is likely to be one of the abuses that figures in this world (Tizard and Phoenix, 1993, p. 106) and may be extremely destructive to self-esteem as well as physically harmful (Onwurah, 1988; Barter, 1998). The direct work again needs to begin with the worker (parent/ carer/professional) who needs to challenge 'that piece of the oppressor which is planted deep within each of us' (Lorde, 1984 p. 123) so that racist language and/or actions do not further diminish the child's safety and negate any positive outcome of the direct work. The circle of safety then needs to be widened to include others directly working with the child – relatives, friends, colleagues, neighbours, schools and so on. However, as racism is unlikely to be abolished or completely buffered, the direct worker needs to be prepared to work with the child around the abuse of racism, employing similar methods as in working with other abuses, namely:

- naming racism and putting it in a structural framework so that the child does not feel guilty or responsible for their experience of racism;
- enabling an expression of the feelings racism may engender e.g. pain, powerlessness, betrayal, anger;
- reducing the feeling of powerlessness of the child by working out strategies to challenge racism with which the child is comfortable; and
- encouraging the network of support and the group identity that contribute to the above.

As well as experiencing racism from white peers and adults, black children with a white parent who are of light skin colour and/or do not identify as black may be excluded and taunted by some black children. The roots of this exclusion lie in the racism targeted at black people, the strategy of some of those who are less visibly black to distance themselves from a black identification, and the preferential treatment sometimes meted out to this "lighter" group by white society (Camper, 1994; Featherston, 1994; Prevatt Goldstein, 1999). The history of this racism and its continuing significance in the wider society and in playground politics contribute to those who are less visibly black or have a white parent sometimes being called upon to demonstrate their solidarity with their black peers. This lack of immediate acceptance into a black group may be isolating for a child who is also receiving racist taunts. The parent/carer/professional (direct worker) needs to:

- acknowledge that this exclusion may happen, without assuming it is widespread or frequent and appreciate that its roots lie in racism;
- enable the child to express their pain, isolation and anger;
- help the child to name this exclusion, understand the reasons for it and how their behaviour may contribute to it;
- help the child to understand the significance of black identification and gain the tools to incorporate this in ways which do not deny their individuality or white parentage; and
- work with others to limit racism, the preference for lighter shades of black, the denial of the importance of black identification as well as to challenge the narrow vision of black which promotes stereotyping and exclusion (hooks, 1991, p. 28)

The methods employed should, as previously, start with the direct worker working with their own attitudes, then incorporate the materials, stories, shared experiences, historical material, references to current events which may help the child gradually acquire an understanding of exclusion and the skills to pre-empt and challenge it. They may need to adopt a more explicit dialogue on the subject if the child's experiences suggest this is necessary. In every case the direct worker needs to be guided by the child's developmental age, coping strategies and level of support systems.

Any direct work with black children with a white parent therefore needs to:

- support a positive self-esteem based on a realistic self-concept of being black with a white parent without assuming this is damaged or the only aspect of self which requires attention;
- start with the attitudes of the parent/carer/worker and work carefully at the child's pace;
- recognise the reality and complexity of abuse (racism and exclusion) and the likely impact and work to reduce these without assuming they are equivalent or the same for every child; and

- be aware that there are likely to be innumerable other experiences, positive and negative, impacting on that child.

Professional contexts of direct work

A concern with self-concept, self-esteem and security is a priority in much direct work with black children with a white parent, particularly that undertaken routinely by parents and carers. This focus on self-esteem and buffering of racism is also found among many other black parents (Peters, 1997). This could be considered to reflect a recognition of the child's need in a racist society rather than pathologisation. Its place in situations of professional intervention e.g. self-harm, destructive behaviour, an experience of abuse, separation, substitute parenting needs to be recognised, not to stereotype and inappropriately intervene (Owusu-Bempah, 1994) but to enrich and focus this professional intervention for the benefit of the children.

Situations of abuse

Abuse is usually defined as physical abuse, sexual abuse, emotional abuse and neglect. A black child with a white parent suffering any of the above is also likely to have the experience of racist abuse. This may draw the child into feeling the additional abuse is to be expected, deserved and that help is unlikely to be forthcoming or straightforward. Children may feel there is no readily available reference group if they have internalised the message that they are unacceptable to both black and white people. Whether the child is abused by a black person or a white person, it complicates for that child the task of valuing their whole self. If the child is abused by a black person and placed in a white substitute home and receives help/direct work from white people only, it may accelerate a process of negative stereotyping of black people and distancing from a black reality. The direct worker needs to first be open to these possibilities and subsequently structure the process of direct work to enable these issues to be worked with, if appropriate to the individual child.

Behavioural difficulties

Behavioural difficulties whether withdrawal and self-harm or aggressive destructive behaviour may be, as with many children, a response to conditions of emotional, racial, sexual and physical abuse. They may also be a response to the particular pressures society imposes on black children with a white parent e.g. they may demonstrate a conforming to the stereotypical expectation of identity confusion and conflict or the adoption of a strong negative role to avoid uncertainty and ambivalence. There may also be an element of conformity to the stereotype of aggressive black youth, more usually associated with African-Caribbean boys, or passive withdrawn black youth, more often associated with South Asian girls (Lawrence, 1982). Again, direct workers need to be open to the complex roots of behavioural difficulties and structure their intervention to enable work with abuse, self-concept and self-esteem to be explored, without assuming that this may always be required.

Separation and loss

In direct work around separation and loss, the fantasies of the child and the feeling that their wishes and behaviour may have caused the situation are often key factors (Fahlberg, 1991). In coming towards self-concept and self-esteem, black children with a white parent may go through many stages of wishful thinking about being white only, black only, different parents, different situations (Tizard and Phoenix, 1993). If the loss occurs during these stages the child may feel they have contributed to it. Direct workers will need to be aware of this possibility and sensitively enable the child to express their range of feelings and fears.

Substitute parenting

It is commonly accepted that children who are parented/cared for away from their birth parents may have to deal with issues of separation and loss (Fahlberg, 1994) and identity (Ryburn, 1995). The experience of being separated and reparented is likely to heighten the developmental tasks around self-concept and self-esteem and care needs to be taken to place the child in the most positive circumstances for developing these. Wilson (1987) suggests that the most positive circumstances may be:

- a black principal carer (mother);

- parents comfortable with their own racial identity;
- parents who see their child as both black and "mixed race";
- parents who recognise racism as a reality that will affect their child and that needs to be fought by group action; and
- a multiracial neighbourhood including children of diverse racial and cultural parentages.

This is supported by some research findings (EYTARN, 1995) and the personal accounts of many (Camper, 1994; Featherston, 1994). Other research findings, including those of Tizard and Phoenix (1993), support principally the multiracial neighbourhood.

Children who are being reparented in all-white homes in all-white neighbourhoods may have high self-esteem. This may be based on a realistic self-concept and result from careful and continuous direct work by parents/carers. Self-esteem may also be based on a denial of blackness (Gill and Jackson, 1983). This may result in a variety of behaviours including skin-scrubbing, derogatory language and behaviour towards black people (Maximé, 1993) but may also co-exist with high academic achievement or apparent social integration (Gill and Jackson, 1983; Simon and Alstein, 1987). Direct work needs to be sensitive to the survival strategies the children have developed, the degree of parental support or resistance, and provide resources including materials, individual work and groupwork at the child's pace. Some children, parented or reparented, will initiate their own structures for direct work at stages when they can take the initiative and/or there is support:

Once able to face [my mother's racism] (and I still deal with the effects) I have made conscious efforts to find out about and value both parts of my heritage.

(Adult 2, EYTARN, 1995, p. 59)

The direct worker

The exploration of direct work around self-concept and self-esteem, around security and in diverse contexts e.g. abuse and separation, give some indication of the values and skills needed by the direct worker. This may be useful in the selection and training of carers and professional workers and in facilitating the support and development needs of all those (parents/carers/professionals) working with black children with a white parent. The areas that it would be helpful for workers to develop may be summarised as:

- their relationship with the child and those significant to the child;
- their appreciation of the strengths of the child and possibilities of resolution of any difficulties now or later;
- their knowledge of their own value system on self-concept, self-esteem, "race", racism, parenting and their commitment to question and develop these;
- their ability to understand the complex developmental tasks that society has imposed on the black child with a white parent, without pathologising the child or minimising the range of other issues and situations in which the child will be involved;
- their awareness of the significance of their colour and "racial" identity to the child and significant others;
- their skill at balancing the urgency of positive outcomes and the need to work at the child's pace; and
- their skill in working with those significant to the child.

Professional workers will additionally need to take account of whether the primary carer(s) identify as white or black, take a political stance on racism, or locate themselves in a black supportive network, all significant to the self-concept and self-esteem of the child, as indicated by the research (Wilson, 1987; Banks, 1992; Tizard and Phoenix, 1993; Younge, 1994; EYTARN, 1995). The primary carer's position as birth parent or alternative/substitute parent may also suggest that there will be different issues to consider in working together. Banks' research (1992) highlights a group of birth mothers, white, ostracised because of their black children, and carrying negative resonances about black people because of their experiences with their black partners. Direct work with the children can best take place if work is done with these parents about their negativity about black people and its impact on the children as the main carer is likely to be the principal and most influential direct worker with the children. However, other research has highlighted white birth parents who are fully engaged in direct work with their children on these issues and who may well guide the professional workers:

I am always positive about their colour and do not accept any
negative attitudes. We are limited in the places that we can live as I
would never consider taking my children to live in an all white society.
(Parent 3 in EYTARN, 1995, p. 35)

In working with those involved in reparenting, issues around childless-
ness, around rescue, around need and ownership may figure independently or in conjunction with negativity towards black people. Mullender
and Miller's project on groupwork with black children in care (1985)
demonstrated the resistance of some white carers and the importance of
working directly with them. Children in residential establishments may
receive negative messages, not only from the workers but also from their
peer group, and work with both, separately and jointly, may be the way
forward in the context of sound policy and practice guidelines.

Many black primary carers may, like some white primary carers,
already be engaged in positive direct work with their children:

I have worked on myself and have read a lot... My youngest
daughter wanted to have long blonde straight hair... and we talked
and tried to work through it. (Parent 11 in EYTARN, 1995, p. 41)

Their efforts should be valued rather than taken for granted. There will
be other black parents who are unaware e.g. the many non-politicised
black parents in Tizard and Phoenix's (1993) study. These parents'
survival strategies may need careful challenging so that they can support
the direct work with their child.

The professional direct worker is more likely to be working with
substitute carers and white mothers of black children with a white parent,
the latter being more likely to access social services departments than
black parents (Barn, Sinclair and Ferdinand, 1997). Work with all parents/
carers need to be aware of the likely different experiences and perspectives, open to their strengths, and appropriately challenging in order to
engage them as allies in direct work with their children.

Summary and conclusion

This chapter has identified the developmental tasks that are specific to
the black child with a white parent and which may impinge on all direct

work with them: the tasks of building positive self-esteem based on a realistic self-concept that can manage the duality of that which society has constructed as opposites, white and black; and the task of resisting racist abuse and exclusion. It has provided a framework for identifying both how direct work may focus explicitly on these, and how these may be explored in interventions around abuse, behavioural difficulties, separation and substitute parenting, if appropriate. This framework is relevant to all directly working with black children with a white parent – parents, carers and professionals – and can be summarised as:

- addressing the attitudes and values of the direct worker (parent/carer/ professional);
- consistently offering the child an environment which encourages a valuing of black and white people;
- a recognition that being black with a white parent is normal, and which allows the child some safety from abuse by naming and challenging racism and exclusion ;
- accepting multiplicity, change and uncertainty in the child's develop- ment of "racial" self-concepts and self-esteem while structuring the environment to provide the social and political context;
- recognising the diversity and individuality of each child, valuing each child with their diverse experiences and numerous self-concepts around age, religion, ethnicity, gender and so on; and
- while maintaining all the above, if necessary, explicitly challenging unrealistic self-concepts, negative self-esteem, and collusion with racism at a pace that is sensitive to the child's age, understanding and support systems.

This chapter also explored the knowledge, values and skills, needed by the direct worker to facilitate the above. The guidelines on the attributes needed by the worker and on the framework for the direct work needed by the children are offered to develop good practice, without losing sight of the success with which many workers (parents/carers/pro- fessional workers) and many children accomplish these tasks:

Being of mixed parentage has given me a strong sense of my own identity, although developing it has been a struggle but with a strong sense of victory at the outcome. (Adult 4 in EYTARN, 1995, p. 59)

References

Association of Black Social Workers and Allied Professionals, (1983) *Black children in Care: Evidence to the House of Commons Social Services Committee*, ABSWAP.

Banks, N. (1992) 'Some considerations of 'racial' identification and self-esteem when working with mixed ethnicity children and their mothers as social services clients'. In *Social Services Research, Birmingham University*, 3.

Barter, C. (1998) *Protecting Children from Racism and Racial Abuse*, NSPCC.

Barn, R. (1993) *Black Children in the Public Care System*, London: BAAF/ Batsford.

Barn, R. Sinclair, R. and Ferdinand, D. (1997) *Acting on Principle*, London: BAAF.

Barn, R. (1999) 'White mothers, mixed-parentage children and child welfare'. In *British Journal of Social Work*, 29:2.

Bebbington, A. and Miles, J. (1989) 'The background of children who enter local authority care'. In *British Journal of Social Work*, 19:5, pp 349–69.

Brah, A. (1992) 'Difference, diversity, differentiation'. In Donald, J. and Rattansi, A. (eds) *'Race', Culture and Difference*, Sage.

Burman, E. (1994) *Deconstructing Developmental Psychology*, London: Routledge.

Butt, J. and Mirza, K. (1996) *Social Care and Black Communities*, Race Equality Unit.

Camper, C. (1994) *Miscegenation Blues*, Vision Press.

Derman-Sparks, L., Higa, T. C. and Sparks, B. (1980) 'Suggestions for developing positive racial attitudes'. In *Council on Interracial Books for Children*, 11:3 and 4.

Dutton, E. (1995) *Direct Work with Children in New Families*, Barnardo's, unpublished.

EYTARN (Early Years Trainers Anti Racist Network) (1995) *The Best of Both Worlds, Celebrating Mixed Parentage*, EYTARN.

Fahlberg, V. (1994) *A Child's Journey through Placement*, London: BAAF.

Featherston, E. (1994) *Skin Deep*, The Crossing Press.

Gill, O. and Jackson, B. (1983) *Adoption and Race*, London: Batsford/BAAF.

Green, H. (1994) 'This piece done, I shall be renamed'. In Camper (ed) *Miscegenation Blues*, Vision Press.

hooks, b. (1991) *Yearning*, Turnaround.

Jackson, J. S., McCullough, W. R. and Gurin, G. (1997) 'Family, Socialization, Environment and Identity in Black Americans'. In McAdoo, H. P. *Black Families*, Sage.

Jayaweera, H. (1993) 'Racial disadvantage and ethnic identity: the experiences of Afro-Caribbean women in a British city'. In *New Community*, 19.

Lawrence, E. (1982) 'In the midst of plenty the fool is hungry'. In Centre for Contemporary Cultural Studies, *The Empire Strikes Back*, Hutchinson.

Lorde, A. (1984) *Sister Outsider*, Crossing Press.

Mama, A. (1995) *Beyond the Masks*, London: Routledge.

Maximé, J. (1993) 'The importance of racial identity for the psychological well-being of black children'. In *ACCP Review and Newsletter*, 15:4.

McNeilly, K. N. (1994) 'Don't mix me up'. In Camper (ed) *Miscegenation Blues*, Vision Press.

Miles, R. (1994) 'Explaining racism in contemporary Europe', in Rattansi, A. and Westwood, S. Polity Press (eds) *Racism, Modernity Identity*.

Modood, T. (1988) ' "Black" racial equality and Asian identity'. In *New Community*, 14:3.

Modood, T., Beishon, S. and Virdee, S. (1997) *Ethnic Minority Families*, Policy Studies Institute.

Mullender, A. and Miller, D. (1985) 'The Ebony Group: Black children in white foster homes'. In *Adoption and Fostering*, 9.

Onwurah, N. A. and Onwurah, H. K. (1988) *Coffee Coloured Children*, Albany Videos.

Owen, D. (1996) 'Black-other: The melting pot'. In Peach, C. (ed) *Ethnicity in the 1991 Census*, OPCS.

Owen, D. (1994) *Black people in Great Britain: Social and economic circumstances, 1991 Census*, Statistical paper No. 6, University of Warwick: Centre for Research in Ethnic Relations.

Phoenix, A. and Owen, C. (1996) 'From miscegenation to hybridity: mixed relationships and mixed-parentage in profile'. In Bernstein, B. and Brannen, J. (eds) *Children, Research and Policy*, Taylor and Francis.

Owusu-Bempah, J. 'Race, self-identity and social work'. In *British Journal of Social Work*, 24, pp. 123–36.

Paulse, M. (1994) 'Commingled'. In Camper (ed) *Miscegenation Blues*, Vision Press.

Peters, M. F. (1997) 'Historical note: Parenting of young children in black families'. In McAdoo, H. P. (ed) *Black Families*, Sage.

Prevatt Goldstein, B. (1997) 'A Mixed Response! Services to black children of mixed parentage'. In *Seminar Papers*, London: BAAF.

Prevatt Goldstein, B. (1999, forthcoming) 'Black with one parent: A positive and achievable identity'. In *British Journal of Social Work*, London: London.

Rowe, J., Hundleby, M. and Garnett, L. (1989) *Child Care Now*, London: BAAF.

Ryburn, M. (1995) 'Adopted children identity and information needs'. In *Children and Society*, 9:3.

Simon, R. and Alstein, H. (1987) *Transracial Adoptees and their Families: A Study of Identity and Commitment*, Praeger.

Small, J. (1986) 'Transracial placements: Conflicts and contradictions'. In Ahmed, S., Cheetham, J. and Small, J. *Social Work with Black Children and their families*, London: BAAF/Batsford.

Tizard, B. and Phoenix, A. (1993) *Black, White or Mixed Race?* London: Routledge.

Wilson, A. (1987) *Mixed Race Children: A study of identity*, Allen and Unwin.

Woollett, A., Marshall, H., Nocoloson, P. and Dosanjh, N. (1994) 'Impact of Gender and Context in the Accounts of Women Bringing up Children in East London'. In Bhavnani, K. K. and Phoenix, A. *Shifting Identities, Shifting Racisms*, Sage.

Younge, G. (1994) 'Mixed Blessings'. In *The Guardian*, 6 December.

5 Anti-discriminatory issues in child protection

Bharti Dhir

Introduction

This chapter explores the key issues in anti-discriminatory child protection practice. It is divided into three parts. The first part focuses upon the process of assessment in the context of current child care legislation. The second consists of a discussion of two case studies involving black children in which child protection issues are raised in respect of anti-discriminatory practice. The third part provides some general guidelines in the implementation of anti-discriminatory practice. I would like to state at the start that the opinions offered in this article are my own and not necessarily those of the local authority where I work.

Assessment: A legal and practice perspective

Much has been said about the 1989 Children Act identifying the need to ensure that a child's racial, cultural, linguistic and religious background is taken into account in social work decision-making. The fact that these issues are addressed legally promises to be an encouraging sign paving the way for a further reinforcement of anti-discriminatory values in practice.

Hitherto, within the child protection arena, many of us who are black practitioners and managers were advised in our assessments by guidance offered by the Department of Health (DoH) in the "orange" book, *Protecting Children: A guide for social workers undertaking a comprehensive assessment*. This manual, as anyone practising child protection or intending to knows, is usually held up as the "Bible" of good assessment. Certainly I, along with many colleagues, have poured over it trying to assess which "category" a family or individual belonged to and also trying to determine the checklist of questions that would enable a comprehensive assessment of the family based on "good" practice. Again, I was cheered by the fact that the manual addressed the issues of "race" and culture. It stated that:

No culture sanctions extreme harm to a child . . . A balanced assess-
ment must incorporate a cultural perspective but guard against being
oversensitive to cultural issues at the expense of promoting the safety
and well being of the child. (DoH, 1988:13)

It also advised practitioners to take note of families that may be under particular stress due to racial harassment from the community.

However, as I increasingly began to assess the guidance from a black perspective, I began to be aware that many of the questions I was being encouraged to ask were Eurocentric in their assumptions. By Eurocentric I mean:

Looking at, exclusively valuing and interpreting the world through the
eyes and experiences of white Europeans. This includes, for example,
the presentation and interpretation of historical events; defining of
"correct" methods of child rearing and organising family life; seeing
Europe as the centre of the world. (Macdonald, 1991: p. VI)

Our assessments were therefore fundamentally flawed because whilst we were workers from the same cultural background as the family some-times, and whilst some of us were aware of racial issues that the family might be experiencing, many of us still *adopted* the Eurocentric style of questioning that the guidance advised us to address. Those workers who did not adopt that style of questioning had to justify their lack of assess-ment to their supervisors with the knowledge that their competence would be questioned. To say that some questions were inappropriate was just not acceptable in the system most of us operated in within social services. For example, questions on the eye contact the child might have with an adult, or the behaviour a child exhibits in front of some adults, could lead to erroneous assumptions being made about the child's interaction with the adults in his or her life, if many of us were unaware of various cultural nuances. Unfortunately many of us *were* unaware. The guidance ignored some of the complex dynamics that might arise from perceived racism within some of the questions.

Similarly, *Working Together under the Children Act 1989*, addressed various facets of child protection work such as the roles of Area Child

Protection Committees and various organisations and individuals in child protection work and yet many of us would argue that it has failed to provide an integral anti-racist or anti-discriminatory dimension. This is despite its undertaking that:

The basis of an effective child protection service must be that of professionals and individual agencies working together with a shared mutual understanding of aims, objectives and what is good practice. This should take in account the sensitive issues associated with gender, race, culture and disability. (DoH, 1991:25)

Returning to the Children Act, whilst I applauded the addressing of issues of "race", culture, language and religion in the Children Act, that sense of elation was also overshadowed by a sense of pessimism. If that aspect of the Children Act were to be challenged, my feeling is that it could be the first provision to go. Failing that, it would perhaps be amended to such a degree that compromises eventually reached would ensure that factors such as a child's religious, racial, linguistic and cultural background would be viewed as unimportant and a resultant mockery made of such issues. More importantly, in considering the welfare of the child and stressing that this is paramount, the Act does not define that a child's, culture, "race", language or religion all play a crucial role in determining that child's welfare. It has to be pointed out therefore:

... The Children Act may end up with little or no impact in promoting the welfare and protecting the interests of the Black child [if these] ... are left to the rhetoric of the Act and not transferred into social work action. (Macdonald, 1991: p. VIII)

I still hope that issues relating to "race" and culture of the child will not be confined solely to placement issues.

In the next part, I discuss two cases and endeavour to illustrate what is meant by anti-discriminatory practice. Each case highlights the types of issues that could arise in terms of identity and the practice implications when one is considering the racial, cultural, linguistic and religious background of the children. In communicating with children and in upholding the values of anti-discriminatory practice, it is important to hold onto the belief that what one is attempting to do is possible even when one is facing the "seemingly impossible".

Pre-assessment thoughts

My initial starting point, therefore, has to be myself as practitioner:

- What are my feelings about anti-racism or anti-discrimination?
- Can I identify my prejudices?
- What are my concerns?
- Do I believe that racial, religious, linguistic and cultural values are important when I am addressing a family or a child that I am working with?

Anti-discriminatory practice encourages a holistic *positive* approach embracing an individual's "race", gender, sexuality, class, religion, and culture. When assessing and providing a service, the above factors must all be taken into account to ensure that all needs are met and there is not a shortfall in the service provided ultimately.

If I am not sure about my perspective on these issues, then it could be argued that when I am challenged in any form, it could be easy for me to search for a compromise or to back down. There are practitioners who still argue that anti-discriminatory practice is an ideological piece of rhetoric and impossible to implement. This issue is explored further in the two cases discussed below. I would argue that some colleagues may scorn the importance of some issues raised by the two children discussed in the cases, as being "politically correct". In response I would state that many of us who have worked with and are still working with black children who have been abused, will be familiar with the type of issues that a child may struggle with, particularly if that child is from a different racial and cultural background. Most of us will be very familiar with the situation presented by Desmond and Yasmin.

It has taken many months for me to examine my own values in terms of child protection and black families and to reach a viewpoint that I felt comfortable with, and which I believed reflected the needs of the child, not only in the short term but also in the long term once that child had left the care system.

Desmond

Desmond was nine years old. He lived with his mother and step-father. Desmond's mother had remarried when he was five years old. She came to social services following the birth of a daughter, who, at the time she referred herself, was nearly one year old. Desmond's mother was expressing concern about his "bad behaviour" ever since her marriage, but the behaviour had escalated since the birth of the daughter. Both parents were at their wit's end and Desmond's step-father had given her an ultimatum. Either Desmond was "sorted out" or he would leave. He was said to be constantly criticising Desmond and seemed to dislike him intensely. Desmond's mother was afraid that he would hurt Desmond badly as he had already hit him quite badly in the past and she had three requests:

1. Could we remove Desmond and place him in care, so that the family could have a break from him?
2. Could we find out the reason for his behaviour?
3. Could we stop the behaviour before he was returned home?

"Bad" behaviour was eventually clarified as Desmond wetting and soiling himself; stealing from school and various family friends; and a conviction on the parents' part that he could physically abuse the younger child. This thought stemmed from the fact that he was found the previous day writing on the books at school and telling his friends that he was going to kill his sister and giving graphic descriptions of how he was going to do it. So afraid were they of what he might do, that Desmond was kept apart from her and no interaction was allowed between the two. Clearly there was an emotional abuse issue and there were concerns for Desmond's safety if he remained at home with his stepfather due to the physical abuse he had suffered from him previously.

The case was complex and raised many issues. I intend to highlight the issues in respect of anti-discriminatory practice. Desmond's mother had wanted a placement with a Nigerian family. If this was not possible, she asked that he was placed in any African family where they would have sympathy with his religious background and encourage his religious beliefs: the family was Catholic. She was afraid of him being placed anywhere that could lead to a loss of his beliefs or racial identity. She felt that an African or black family would at least empathise with the cultural background Desmond came from. In considering her requests, we were putting into effect one of the principles of anti-discriminatory practice, that is, basically listening to her and taking seriously her views on the type of placement she wanted.

At this stage Desmond was able to identify with his mother on these issues and was very anxious not to lose contact with his family. The only Nigerian foster carers lived near the family and Desmond's mother was embarrassed about them finding out her details, so we had to look further afield. Even if we found a family, we had to consider the implications of placing Desmond with them. For example, even if a family were able to cope with his wetting and soiling, if Desmond was thinking of killing a younger child it meant possible risk to other children in the family. Desmond needed a thorough assessment.

Eventually Desmond was placed in a residential unit that specialised in assessing children with the type of behavioural concerns that Desmond was alleged to present. Every effort was made to find foster carers from a similar racial background as the child. However, we were unsuccessful primarily because carers did not want the risk of taking on a child with Desmond's behaviour.

The residential unit in which Desmond was placed had no black staff and was situated in a predominantly white area. Before placing Desmond with them, it was felt crucial to ascertain their views in respect of anti-racist and anti-discriminatory practice. Was this addressed in their policies and procedures? I needed to know that issues in respect of Desmond's "race" and culture would not be ignored. Before Desmond was placed with the unit, besides other issues, a contractual agreement was set up between the local authority, parent, child and unit respectively. The unit promised that they would uphold the following:

1. Desmond would be taken to a local Catholic church each week and his religious identity maintained.
2. The unit had a policy of encouraging a varied diet, so even when black children were not resident, they ensured that staff and all children were given meals from different cultures twice weekly. They asked for

recipes so their cook could cook some of Desmond's favourite Nigerian dishes.

3. Measures were identified to deal with racist abuse directed at Desmond by other children i.e. the director of the unit asserted that, in the event of racial harassment/abuse, the child who was committing the offence would be taken aside and told why his or her behaviour was wrong and what action would be taken if he or she persisted. This could mean removal to another of the unit's homes or expulsion, with notice being given for the reason for expulsion.

These factors served to allay Desmond's mother's fears of his losing his identity. She felt the unit understood what the issues were. We also ascertained the unit's policy on racism from staff.

Within a week of being placed in the unit, Desmond had tested some of the guidelines. On the day a Nigerian dish was cooked, Desmond declared to staff and residents that he hated African food and only loved English food. (Interestingly, Desmond's main worry prior to being placed in the unit was that he would not be able to eat his favourite Nigerian dishes while he was there.) Staff were equally quick to point out what they loved about Nigerian food thus quelling any possible objections from both Desmond and other children. By the time Desmond left the unit approximately eight weeks later, he was instructing the cook on how to make more Nigerian dishes, and taking great pride in the fact that his recipes were being tried and tested. Like many black children, when placed in a white establishment, Desmond was quick to start neglecting his diet for fear of ridicule and/or abuse from other children. Had this not been challenged constructively, I believe he would have rejected his diet ultimately.

Another example was that of Desmond's language. The second time his mother visited, Desmond refused to answer her in Yoruba and was clearly embarrassed that she could not speak English fluently. On this occasion, although distressed by this, she refused to answer or respond in English. Both mother and son sat in silence. Eventually Desmond became frustrated by this. On the third and subsequent visits, he spoke in Yoruba to his mother. The key worker spent some time in her sessions addressing this issue and praising the positive aspects of being able to speak more than one language. By encouraging Desmond to continue speaking to his mother in Yoruba, they maintained the closeness that mother and son had. It could so easily have been lost.

Once Desmond's assessment period was over it was possible to place him with an African family. I believe it was the fact that careful attention had been given to the racial issues that might arise and how to deal with them that enabled this. I know many cases where that has not happened and a child has firmly rejected a placement with any black family, preferring to be placed with a white family.

The assessment period was also useful in that it dealt with the other issues relating to possible abuse. Once within the placement, Desmond stopped wetting and soiling himself. As stated the issues were complex. Had the parents exaggerated in order to have him accommodated? Why did he soil himself at home and not the unit?

These were all questions that were addressed. Even when Desmond was placed with a foster family, soiling and abuse did not become an issue. Desmond was eventually rehabilitated at home, once we tried to engage his mother and stepfather to address the various conflictual issues they faced in their relationship. Issues addressed were:

1. what they each felt about Desmond respectively;
2. what they felt about one another; and
3. their belief about physical abuse and how they would deal with what Desmond was going through in terms of a new reconstituted family.

The placement with the African foster family was very successful. Although the residential unit had been supportive Desmond's mother felt more at ease being in a black environment. She was able to speak in confidence to the foster carer about aspects of her relationship with her husband which she felt unable to share with me (single, young, female and a part of the system) or with white workers from the unit. Before placing Desmond with the family, once again we drew up a contractual agreement stressing not only the rules of the house, but that every effort would be made to retain his religious and cultural identity. The foster family respected this and did not impose their values on Desmond or his mother. This enabled both mother and son to trust them and value their professionalism as foster carers.

Operating within an anti-racist and anti-discriminatory framework facilitated the successful rehabilitation of Desmond with his own family. The marginalisation of "race" and ethnicity can exacerbate matters and lead to black children remaining in the care system (Barn, 1993). In this case example, careful consideration was given to anti-racist and anti-discriminatory practice in the process of assessment, in finding a suitable placement, in working with the residential unit, and in the successful rehabilitation of the child.

Yasmin

Yasmin was a 13-year-old girl who was sexually and physically abused by her brother. On disclosing this, she was rejected by her immediate family. Eventually, it transpired that there were members of the extended family network who believed Yasmin and supported her. They came to offer her a home and she resolutely refused all offers including any placement with a black family.

The case of Yasmin illustrates some of the effects of both abuse and racism. How both these factors need to be considered will be explained further, but it is important to stress that in communicating and working with children who have been abused, a holistic approach needs to be adopted. By this, the child or young person or family needs to be seen in the context of "race", class, culture, language, religion, sex and sexuality. Some forms of abuse, especially in respect of the above, may already have started the eroding process before the child was subject to physical and or sexual abuse. The latter compounds the process that has already begun. In Yasmin's case, racial prejudice had already begun the rot of "chipping" away at her self-esteem.

Great sensitivity had to be adopted when communicating and working with Yasmin. Yasmin needed to be assured that she was not to blame for the abuse, that the responsibility for the abuse lay with the abuser. She needed to be advised that it was not her fault she had been abused and that feelings of guilt, anger and shame were natural occurrences following the abuse. She also needed to know that the power lay with the abuser. The approach followed applied the basic tenets of a feminist model regarding sexual abuse relating to children. I used this approach chiefly because I felt comfortable with the principles it encouraged. I had studied other approaches in respect of sexual abuse and felt uneasy at the implications of blame and responsibility that some advocate in respect of children and families subject to abuse.

I had to try and convey to Yasmin that in no way was she responsible for the abuse and that her cultural and familial systems were not dysfunctional. The abuse occurred as a result of one adult person exploiting a younger, vulnerable child and a person who knew the power he had over the child.

Had I started to look at the family, or the cultural system, I would have ventured along the dangerous path of looking at Yasmin's family and cultural system in a negative and ultimately racist light. By enabling her to see the abuse as an *individual* act, she found it difficult to continue blaming the whole system (familial, cultural and religious) as the cause of abuse and one which sanctioned it. The common and basic themes in therapeutic work with children who have been abused were rendered more complex because of some of the cultural connotations.

She found it difficult, for example, to grasp the concept that she was not to blame or responsible for the abuse. She argued that all her life she had been taught to dress in a certain way and eat in a certain way. She had been zealous in her religious duties. Deviating from the above, she felt, would lead to retribution of sorts. It took a long time for Yasmin to believe that she was not to blame or responsible for the abuse. She constantly questioned whether it was the way she had dressed on particular occasions, or the way she laughed or looked at her brother, that led to the abuse. She felt she must have done something to warrant it and constantly came up with reasons to explain why she felt this way. It also took time to explore her sense of shame and betrayal without colluding with the negative attitude she held towards her family and community which stemmed from her abuse.

Yasmin felt strongly about the fact that she had done everything she could to uphold the moral and ethical codes of a young Muslim girl. She felt intense anger at the "hypocritical" values she felt she had been subjected to, and the fact that the family should reject her when they should have been rejecting her brother, who had broken the moral and ethical codes.

The themes in communicating with Yasmin were basically two-fold. Not only did I have to address what the abuse meant as a part of the natural healing process, but also what the abuse meant from a cultural perspective, and what that healing process entailed. For example, Yasmin felt anger and grief at losing her childhood. In working with her, one had to address that but also the anger and grief at losing a whole family and community.

When Yasmin's anger transferred itself to the community, she stated she would rather go to a white family than a black family as 'all black families are hypocrites'. The work then took on another meaning. Yasmin was asked to consider that whilst the abuse and subsequent events following disclosure may, on the face of it, be the causal factors in rejecting herself, her family and community, she had been subject to other forms of abuse long before then. To do this, we looked at the effects of racism. When did she first become aware of its existence? What were the incidents and how did they impinge on her self-worth? How did the racist incidents make her feel about herself, her family, her community and religion?

Yasmin recalled an incident when she was seven years old which had left her feeling ashamed of herself and wishing she were born white. Once Yasmin was able to trace that the gradual erosion of her identity had begun then, she was able to address why she felt so strongly embittered towards her family and community. She felt there was a need to be accepted by the "other". If her own family and community did not want her, then she desperately sought acceptance by a white family. Added to this were complex issues related to revenge. She wanted to hurt her family and, by going to a white establishment or family, she knew she could succeed in this. It was also an attempt to gain some measure of control and power for herself.

Yasmin was encouraged to explore the advantages and disadvantages of a placement in a white family and a black family. Both options were explored in realistic terms. Whatever choice she made eventually had to be made in the context of her understanding as fully as possible what the implications would be for her. These issues were also explored in respect of the long-term implications once she had left the care system, that is, survival skills in case she was on her own, perhaps, and the awareness that she would feel isolated and lonely. How would she celebrate her religious festivals? Where would she fit in this society? Whilst a child is in the care system, it is easy for that child to be lulled into a false sense of security about the support he or she believes they will continue to receive. Black And In Care's (BIC) research indicates that over 70 per cent of black children return home of their own accord once they leave the care system. This is in cases where no rehabilitation was considered possible by the social workers whilst those children were in care. Racism, isolation and a feeling of "not belonging anywhere" can hit hard once one has left the care system.

Guidelines for anti-discriminatory practice

In this final part, I offer some guidelines on what constitutes anti-discriminatory practice in child protection generally. Virdee (1992) states that:

An awareness and understanding of institutional racism and dis-crimination experienced by Black and ethnic minority groups and individuals in British society is crucial, in terms of how ideology, attitudes and values have undermined and devalued their culture, norms, values, life-style and child-rearing practices. (Virdee, 1992:51)

Had I not had this understanding I would not have been able to compre-hend why Desmond's mother was so insistent on the placement meeting his racial and cultural needs; neither would I have insisted upon these issues being part of the contractual agreement with the unit.

Another factor that I needed to consider in terms of anti-discrimina-tory practice was that of the child's identity. In order to implement an anti-discriminatory approach it is essential to adopt a holistic approach in one's work. Margaret Kennedy, who has done extensive work with deaf children who have been abused, has highlighted the importance of working not only with the effects of the abuse, but also the abuse the child may have been subjected to as a result of his or her disability. The effects of racism on a child's sense of identity have been well documented (Ahmed, 1986; Ahmad, 1990). Ahmad quotes David Milner's study on the effects of racism. She points out that:

The evidence suggests that Black children are more, rather than less,

aware of racial differences and their significance than white children.
(Ahmad, 1990:156)

White children are generally surrounded by images to value and identify with, whilst black children are normally subject to negative images, for example, the association of blackness with evil. Children are also able to pick up derogatory messages from people around them. It is therefore not unusual to find black children asking to be placed with white families. There may be other more complex reasons for the request, but it is essential that the worker understands the fundamental impact of racism and how it can impinge upon a child's sense of self-worth from an early age. Work with the child must also address the impact of negative messages in respect of that child or young person's "race", culture, sexuality, disability, religion or class. In Yasmin's case I had to be aware that,

. . . the so-called crisis of cultural conflict may sometimes be masking a crisis of racial identity and self-image . . . (Ahmed *et al*, 1986:146)

Additionally, other factors that must be considered in order to promote anti-discriminatory practice in child protection, both in the investigative context and in the general sense, are as follows:

The referral form must reflect the racial, cultural, religious and linguistic background of the child/family being referred.

In terms of language (if English is not the first language spoken), steps must be taken to ensure that the service user understands the following:

- The reasons they have been referred.
- Why two agencies have to intervene i.e police and social services and their roles, goals and objectives.
- All procedures must be explained as must the possible outcome of both agencies' intervention. This is equally important.
- An interpreter must be appointed and, as far as possible, should be independent of the family. In cases of difficulty, the interpreters can be used from the family's religious, social or personal network. It is important to work in partnership with the family over the choice of interpreter. Children should never be used as interpreters.
- All written or verbal communication must be translated into the

family's language to ensure that they understand exactly what is happening and why.

- The family's right to have a legal representative should be made clear throughout the process. It should also be explained why it may be in their interest to have this service.
- Access must be given to the complaints procedure of the local authority at the start of the investigation.
- The worker must ensure that all references to the racial, cultural and religious background have direct factual relevance to the intervention. If not, then these references should be avoided as they are merely opinions of the worker.
- Any information that the family offers by way of cultural and/or religious explanations for any act being committed must be checked with colleagues or voluntary and religious organisations reflecting the ethnic background the family come from. This will enable a fairer assessment of the situation. Confidentiality and anonymity must be preserved at all times.
- Workers' records must be factual and written with a view that service users have a right of access to the file.
- Workers must explore with the family how the outcome of any investigation could affect the child/family within the community from a cultural viewpoint.
- Workers should be aware of preconceived ideas regarding cultural and religious factors.
- Workers should be conscious at all times of the law in relation to child protection issues. Where cultural and religious practices conflict with the law the latter should prevail.
- Workers must be aware of what is written in the authority's equal opportunity policy and the aims and the objectives of their intervention in relation to this.
- Workers must be aware that different communities have differing perceptions and experiences of police intervention. Sensitivity to these issues should be considered in meetings where the police are involved.

Conclusion

The discussion presented here is brief and I have only offered an outline of some of the issues that could arise when one is working with black children and young people. Justice has not been done to the complexity of the cases and the many issues that have to be addressed, besides the ones mentioned here. In discussing the cases of Desmond and Yasmin, I hope I have conveyed that anti-discriminatory values in practice need not be impossible to achieve, and that it is possible to address issues related to abuse generally in conjunction with the cultural implications too.

Note

The names used in the case studies have been changed to preserve anonymity.

References

Ahmad, B. (1990) *Black Perspectives in Social Work*, London: Venture Press.

Ahmed, S., Cheetham, J. and Small, J., (eds) (1986) *Social Work with Black Children and their Families*, London: BAAF/Batsford.

Barn, R. (1993) *Black Children in the Public Care System*, London: BAAF/Batsford.

Black and In Care (BIC) (1994) *Black and in Care: Conference Report*, London: Blackrose Press.

Department of Health (1988) *Protecting Children: A guide for social workers undertaking a comprehensive assessment*, London: HMSO.

Department of Health (1991) *Working Together under the Children Act 1989: A guide to arrangements for inter-agency co-operation for the protection of children from abuse*, London: HMSO.

Family Rights Group (1991) *The Children Act 1989: working in partnership with families, A Reader*, London: HMSO.

Macdonald, S. (1991) *All Equal Under the Act*, London: REU/NISW.

Virdee, G. (1992) 'Issues of ethnicity and participation'. In Thoburn, J. (ed) *Involving Families in Child Protection*, University of East Anglia.

6 Communicating with and assessing black children

Aminah Husain Sumpton

This chapter focuses upon specific ways of working with black children. It first examines the different issues of concern to both black and white workers, which need to be acknowledged and "owned" before effective communication can be achieved with black children. The need for detail and accuracy in defining "background" is then addressed with specific reference to "race", culture, religion and language. Key people, tools and methods of assessment are then considered so that a programme of work may be identified for the black child.

Acknowledgement of self – the worker

All workers require ongoing training to promote personal and professional development. For working with black children, this is of course pertinent to both black and white workers. The following are some typical issues which can and do arise.

"Defining self" in relation to name, "race", and country of origin

Those familiar with different religions and culture may deduce an individual's origins correctly. Names can take on a different perspective when they are shortened, changed or abbreviated as in "nick-names". Sometimes, however, this is carried out with a view (conscious or unconscious) of appearing more "Western"/white. For example, Aminah is changed to Amy; Satinder to Sunny; Seriki to Rick. Some Chinese people have a "first" name and a "second"; for example, William Lu. In the UK it is necessary throughout one's life, and in the course of work, to complete forms describing yourself or another person. As a Christian country, the most common question would be "Christian name?", "Surname?", etc. A great deal can be gathered by understanding a person's name, e.g. it can show their religion, nationality and ancestry. Of course, names are often spelt in a slightly different way from country to country – even though the meaning of the name (and its derivation) is the same, e.g. Leila, Laila or Layla.

Thus, the first name a person is known by (forename) is usually a name given by the (child's) parents or close relatives. This name may be combined with another name; traditionally in some cultures it may be the father's first name as well. The surname, or combination of family names, may indicate whether a person is married or belongs to a certain clan, tribe, caste or sect. Care should be taken, therefore, to describe children correctly, accurately and sympathetically. It can be very distressing to be called by the wrong name – and mistakes in this "defining" of a person can prove to be both embarrassing and careless.

Furthermore, the question "Where do you come from?" raises different issues for white and black workers. Do they mean: Where do you live in Britain? Where were you born? How long have you been in Britain? What nationality are you? What is your country of origin? The last three questions are usually more pertinent for black workers.

For those who are of mixed parentage and appear white, further ramifications occur if they define themselves as black; society makes sure that they will feel good about their white parentage but given a positive self identity, they will feel equally positive about their black parentage.

Cultural contact
For white and black workers, it is relevant to acknowledge what part of Britain they have been brought up in and lived, in both childhood and adulthood, and the ethnic mix of that area. Inter-racial harmony can only be achieved where respect and mutual understanding are appreciated in inter-personal terms. The black worker will be faced with different perceptions of themselves according to their own experience of living in areas with a high or low concentration of black people.

Travel or length of stay in countries other than Britain may serve to enlighten one about a different culture, religion and traditions; however, for others it may be superficial contact during a holiday.

Parental views

Parental views and upbringing have an effect on the worker's own perception of racism. White workers brought up in an environment where hostility and prejudice were expressed regarding black people might require particular support to be able to overcome this and work effectively, particularly within black communities. For black workers, this issue would be different, in that their parents/families may either have enabled them to develop a positive black identity, or discouraged them from acknowledging their black identity; the latter group would need counselling and training to support them and promote a positive self-identity before they could work productively, particularly with black communities. Of course, there are also instances of bigotry and prejudice within the black community itself; in all cases this is based on ignorance and can only be addressed by directed training, education and experience.

Religion

In the black communities in the UK, there are nine major religions: Christianity, Islam, Hinduism, Sikhism, Buddhism, Taoism, Confucianism, Zoroastrianism and Jainism. Knowledge of or access to information about other religions, and the cultural implications thereof, is invaluable when working with black children. Workers need to acknowledge and define their own religious beliefs (if any), so that they can place themselves on a spectrum starting from orthodox/fundamentalist at one end, to nominal or non-practising at the other. They then need to examine their views regarding issues – which their [religious] beliefs affect in their work – such as adoption, abortion, homosexuality, divorce, and so on. Even within religious groups there can be bias expressed between different sects or groups. For instance:

Muslim   –   Sunni against Ahmadi/Qadiani

Christian   –   Protestant against Roman Catholic

Hindu   –   Brahmin (priest caste) against Shudras (manual worker/ servant caste)

Strongly held views can influence a worker when, for example, selecting adoptive parents for a child unable to live with birth parents/family. A devout Sunni (Muslim) worker could find it very difficult to select a Qadiani adopter for a Sunni child and support such a placement. This is further illustrated by the knowledge that the Pakistani Government has declared Qadianis as "non-Muslims". The key to such complex issues is to keep the child's individual needs uppermost and seek specialist consultation.

Language
White workers may have the use of languages other than English and these are more likely to be European languages than, for example, Bengali, but there are always exceptions. Some black workers, particularly those from countries like Ghana, Pakistan, China, or Turkey may be bi- or tri-lingual. Such a resource is very valuable as not only is the worker able to communicate directly with children and families, but also interpret for other professionals.

I recently worked effectively with a Ghanaian solicitor in a case where I was appointed guardian *ad litem* involving a Ghanaian birth father and white birth mother, where the solicitor served as a direct link with the family, in explaining to them their alternatives in their language. As she was also familiar with the culture and the country, we were able to circumvent what might have been a more complex and time consuming case. In this case, a young girl aged two was rehabilitated to Ghana to paternal grandparents and this was later confirmed as satisfactory by International Social Services.

Personal relationships with people of a different "race"/religion/ culture
As mentioned above, the population mix in the area of upbringing will have an impact on one's views and experience, and so will the personal relationships (or lack of) with people from other ethnic backgrounds. If such relationships have been cultivated and maintained over a period of time, a positive learning experience will be achieved to promote harmony between black and white communities.

However, if such contact has been actively avoided or shunned, this may have implications for the white or black worker who is isolated from the black or white community respectively, and unable to acknowledge this and work effectively without counselling and/or support.

Anti-racist training and knowledge

Anti-racist training should be provided for workers, white and black, to ensure that this is an integral part of continuous professional development. This should be appraised, monitored and reviewed at regular intervals to emphasise individual personal insights and skills learned or to be learned. A study of the following should be made by all workers:

- International history – a more objective understanding other than a Eurocentric approach should be sought.
- Human geography – a sound knowledge of world maps including the "Peters Projection Map"; elements of ethnology and anthropology; and an appreciation of human rights and living conditions.
- Worldwide religions – and a detailed knowledge of the different branches, sects and groups within the religions.
- Ongoing current affairs.

Experience/exposure to racism

This applies to black workers only – by definition – thus: Racism is a belief that all black people are inferior to white people in relation to their culture, religion, intellect, beliefs, and lifestyles. The direct experience of or exposure to racism, from white adults and/or children, induces feelings such as anger, depression, anxiety and humiliation. Consequently, there is a need for those at the receiving end to be given positive support and/or therapy as appropriate.

Other relevant factors such as health, education, political and social views

Black and white workers must be aware of medical issues of particular relevance to black people. Thalassaemia is found predominantly in people of Greek and Turkish Cypriot origin, and those of East African/Asian origin from the Indian sub-continent. There are well-established organisations that have information and support for such conditions.

For black and white workers, their own political and social views are imperative when considering the effect of this on their own work and relationships. It is very likely that Black workers would have greater knowledge of and direct contact with their country of origin.

Current events in a particular country may have repercussions in

Britain, for example, the continuing unrest and dispute between the Turkish Cypriot and Greek Cypriot communities in Cyprus has an effect on those in Britain.

For some black workers, there is additional pressure from others to have "answers" to difficult political, cultural or even child rearing practices within their own communities.

Care must be taken to ensure that abuse is not hidden behind culture or tradition. A good knowledge of the systems and groupings (e.g. the caste system – Hinduism; tribal groups – Africa; Island groups – Caribbean) is helpful in identifying detail and investigating thoroughly the true implications for the individual concerned.

Defining "race", religion, culture and language
Information to be prepared

There is a requirement for a worker to display both a tenacity and a creative approach in obtaining full and detailed information about a child's background, religion and culture. I have worked on children's cases where neither the child nor the adults were aware of the child's correct name or their country of origin. In one case of a six-year-old girl, Lina, described to me as 'black, possibly African-Caribbean', further enquiries via a maternal grandmother identified her as having a Turkish Cypriot, Muslim father, and a mixed parentage mother who was of Sri Lankan/Roman Catholic/white (Polish/Canadian) origin.

In cases where I have been unfamiliar with a person's "race"/culture, language or religion, I have sought specialist help. For example, via:
- appropriate black professionals
- organisations/local groups/advisory centres
- places of worship
- embassies/high commissions
- ABSWAP (The Association of Black Social Workers and Allied Professionals)
- PPIAS (Parent to Parent Information on Adoption Services)
- The Working Group Against Racism in Children's Resources
- Society of Black Lawyers
- Society of Asian Lawyers

Ali

I was called as an expert witness on cultural issues in the case of a ten-year-old boy called Ali. This case illustrates some of the complexities of placing Asian children. Ali is an Indian Muslim and he was placed in an Asian foster family who were Indian Sikhs.

The local authority was surprised that the placement was disrupting; after all, he had been placed in an "Asian" family. I was able to highlight and detail some of the problems Ali was facing in his everyday life. His sister claimed he smelt 'non-Muslim' (i.e. of bacon). Ali was brought up to eat only halal meat (where the animal is slaughtered in a particular way); no pork or any pork product was eaten or used. The Sikh foster family did not eat halal meat; they ate pork but not beef because the cow is regarded as sacred.

There was also a difference in names. Ali is an Islamic name. Those familiar with Islam would be able to identify Muslim names whether they are from India, Turkey or Nigeria. Singh – the name of the foster family – is the name given to all male members of the Sikh religion.

There were other differences. Ali had short hair but orthodox Sikhs, male and female, do not cut their hair, and Ali's foster father and foster brother wore turbans. Also, as Ali was Muslim, he had been circumcised. Males in the Sikh foster family were not circumcised as this is not their practice.

The Sikh foster family's religious festivals were totally different from those Ali was accustomed to. Brought up as a Muslim, Ali wanted to fast during the month of Ramadan, but found this difficult in a home where he would be the only one. On a particular occasion, the Sikh family were celebrating one of the special annual days, the Martyrdom of Guru Tegh Bahadur, who had been killed by a Muslim ruler in the 17th century because he refused to become a Muslim. Ali was resistant to joining in the celebrations. Ali was also used to going to the Mosque on Fridays. However, the foster family attended the local Gurdwara, the place of worship for Sikhs.

Ali had been to special classes to learn Arabic in order to read the Koran, but the Guru Granth Sahib, the Holy Book of the Sikhs, is in Punjabi and written in Gurmukhi script, a totally different language and script from Arabic. And in the placement, there were also language differences: Ali spoke and wrote Urdu and English; the Sikh family spoke and wrote Punjabi and English, so they were only able to converse in English. Ali's birth mother spoke little English and was unable to communicate with the foster family.

The social services department and the foster family thought adoption was a viable option for Ali. In Sikhism, adoption is practised more often within the wider family or friends and community. In Islam, in strict Sharia law practised by orthodox Muslims, adoption is not recognised.

These many differences described above were pertinent when planning for Ali's future. In fact, the final decision was to seek an Asian Muslim long-term foster placement for Ali with contact with his birth family.

For black people living in Britain, there are "choices" and decisions to be made about following their religion and customs and learning languages. Without a full knowledge of the religion, culture and traditions, a professional working with black families is unable to decide whether the child is functioning as an "orthodox" or non-practising person or somewhere on a scale in between the two.

Unless children have access to knowledge about their heritage, how can they make choices and decisions for themselves, and then later for their own children?

Defining individuals
The case study of Ali showed how important it is to obtain full, clear, detailed information about a child's religion, language and culture. The following checklist is drafted to help a worker ensure that the key facts are known and understood with respect to the individual child. It is crucial that the worker does not make stereotypical comments; workers should look beyond the stereotypes and generalisations about people of different "races", religions and nationality. Indeed, it is a matter of how

an individual fits into their religion/culture and how they choose to express their beliefs; some Sikhs, for instance, choose not to wear a turban and do cut their hair (and shave) both in the UK and India.

The following checklist is a guide to ensure that significant issues are addressed; this should be viewed as a "starter" list and other items added as relevant.

Checklist for obtaining information on the black child

1. Country of origin, town/village; place of birth of child, parents and grandparents.

2. Religion – caste/sect; religious beliefs – pillars of faith, place of worship, holy book, religious law.

3. Language(s)- written/spoken.

4. Child-rearing practices; family traditions (e.g. circumcision, naming); health issues (e.g. use of herbal alternative medicine; blood test for sickle cell anaemia/thalassaemia).

5. Customs/ceremonies (weddings, funerals, use of horoscopes, rituals).

6. Festivals celebrated.

7. Food – diet often linked with religion.

8. Dress/hair – clothes, appearance, tribal markings and jewellery.

9. Adoption – whether legally sanctioned or permitted/recognised by religion.

10. Other relevant issues such as hobbies.

Identifying key people
A detailed study of the child and his or her birth parents and family is essential before individual needs can be identified. The following individuals/groups of people will have vital information to complete the whole picture of the black child, past and present. This will facilitate

future planning so that individual needs may be identified and then effectively communicated.

- *The black child her/himself*
  An essential factor whilst establishing the key people for a black child is to also identify those adults/children who are of the same ethnic, religious, linguistic and cultural background as the child.
- *Birth parents/birth family*
  Members of the extended family and siblings may well have played a significant role in respect of the child.
- *Other significant adults/children*
  In some cultures, family friends may be "vital" people as far as the child is concerned; they may be referred to as "aunty" and/or "uncle". A religious person e.g. a priest, may also have been an important befriender or support for the child/family.
- *Previous carers or sets of carers*
- *Residential carers, foster carers and adoptive parents*
- *Health personnel*
  Health visitors; GP; school nurse; hospital staff.
- *Any specialists*
  e.g. therapist, psychiatrist, psychologist.
- *Education professionals*
  e.g. play group staff, school helpers, teachers, head of school, special interest teacher, college staff.
- *Social services*
  e.g Social worker, family aide
- *Other professionals*
  e.g. Guardian/curator *ad litem*, solicitor, interpreter.

Methods of assessment

Various tools or charts can be used to gather vital information regarding the child, and these can then be interpreted so that the work needed to be done with the child be clearly outlined and planned for (see Figure 1). The four areas to be investigated are:

- The child's own perceptions, feelings and wishes.
- The historical and chronological background of changes in the child's

Figure 1
Elements of assessment

CHILD

- Feelings
- Wishes
- Own views (contribution for report)
- Self-identity

HISTORY

- Health
- Chronology (dates)
- Changes/separations (impact on child)
- No carers (attachments)
- Education

BIRTH PARENTS, FAMILY / SIGNIFICANT OTHERS

- Chronology
- Details of "race", religion, culture, language
- Family tree

CURRENT BEHAVIOUR

- Observed behaviour
- Health issues
- Education: nursery, school
- Contact: birth family
- Attachments: carer and child

life and environment as well as moves and the impact of these on the child, including information regarding health and education.

- Detailed, accurate information regarding birth parents, birth family, and other significant adults and carers.
- Catalogue of observed current behaviour of the child, contact visits and so on.

Flow and impact charts can be used to gather significant information in a clear and concise way.

- Any religious, cultural or linguistic issues need to be recognised from the child's perspective.
- Centile charts can be obtained to indicate growth detail. In November/ December 1994 new centile charts were introduced to replace the Tanner/Whitehouse Standards which were compiled in the 1950s. The new charts confirm that the UK population's mean height has been growing steadily over the last generation. Unfortunately the new charts are based on the indigenous (i.e. white) British population and do not include centiles for minority ethnic communities. The Child Growth Foundation suggests that black children should be assessed bearing in mind the 'generalisation that Asians are smaller and lighter, and Afro-Caribbeans are taller and heavier than the British Caucasian'. Professionals assessing black children in relation to growth should be aware of this information and use centile charts with caution.
- School reports show academic/social adjustment.
- Genograms, ecosystems and other diagrams can be used to illustrate vividly in detail religion, languages, country of origin, place of birth and so on (see Figure 2). This is particularly graphic in children of mixed parentage where more than one religion, language and ethnic origin are represented.
- The views of carers, alongside charts depicting actual behaviour observed, can be analysed whilst considering at what age the child is functioning.
- Finally, once the whole child is defined in terms of his or her needs, ways of meeting those needs can then be formulated. Lifestory work should encompass all the parts of a child's background, describing it

Figure 2
Genography for a black child (an example)

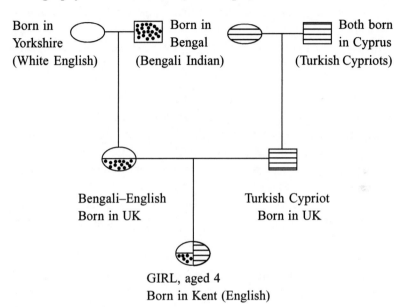

KEY:

	Country of origin	**Religion**	**(Language)**
△	White English	Christian	(English)
△ (dotted)	Bengali Indian	Hindu	(Bengali)
△ (striped)	Turkish Cypriot	Muslim	(Turkish)

in detail so that he or she is fully aware of their uniqueness; then, as an adult, choices can be made regarding practising religion, using language and choosing friends/partners, and so on.

Exploring at the black child's pace
There is often a marked difference, particularly for children in care, between "chronological" age and "mental/emotional" (or functioning)

age; in my experience, most of the time the majority of children I have worked with rarely exhibit the behaviour typical for their age.

Once a rapport has been established with a child, he or she will give an insight into what or who is important for them – a snapshot. This, may be an essential part of the larger jigsaw which will help put together the many pieces to assess the child, and thence understand those individual needs to be addressed.

In many cases, it is evident to me that a black child may never have had a positive image of black adult/carer/parent in their lives. Is it then surprising that they would mistrust black adults or think/feel more comfortable with white workers? A black child who sees him/herself as white has very serious problems – were this a white child seeing himself as black, urgent psychiatric advice would be sought.

Working with black children may be better in individual sessions or in groups; an understanding of their past would facilitate this choice. Some black children will have a clear, strong self-identity and others will need a series of sessions on exploring their links with their country of origin and/or religion. A creative, imaginative formula needs to be constructed for the individual child. For me methods or tools of working could include using:
- computers e.g. using maps, flags and information.
- "play", e.g. multicultural toys, puppets, dolls, games and books
- sports
- art, drawing
- music, dance, drama
- cooking and food (international)
- humour (an essential ingredient)
- worksheets; open-ended questionnaires. e.g. *My three wishes*, *People I'd take on holiday*.

Meeting the black child's needs

All children in care suffer from loss, separation, many changes, and most have had several carers. They may have experienced physical, sexual, emotional abuse and/or neglect. They all carry a heavy burden, a suitcase full. Now all black children, but even more so those in the care system, separated from birth family and their community, carry

Figure 3

Figure 4

THE PARTICULAR NEEDS OF BLACK CHILDREN IN CARE –

this heavy suitcase but in addition to this, they suffer from another type of abuse seldom mentioned in respect to children: racial abuse. This second very heavy suitcase is also full of racism, isolation, discrimination and stereotyping (see Figure 3). Most of the black children I have worked with over the years have suffered from internalising negative images, resulting in self-hate and identity confusion. For example, one child was agitated – she had been called "loo brush" and "cow dung" at school. Some children deny their black identity, and some have never met a "good" black adult. One girl placed in a white family was unable to walk past her neighbour's house without fear of recrimination – the neighbour was overtly racist, for instance, he had refused hospital treatment from a black nurse and had discharged himself.

Over the years, we have learned much about helping children cope with separation and loss. Direct work, various therapies, nurturing and life work, help children to understand who they are, why they have been in care and what their future will be. Black children do need black parents/carers; they also need positive information about their "race", culture, religion, language and traditions. They must have a strong racial identity and learn strategies of how to cope with racism.

For a black child in care, there is the heavy burden of two suitcases: these burdens require reducing. Black children in care will then have the rich experience and pleasure of enjoying their lives and two or more cultures to the maximum, making their choices and sharing those with others (see Figure 4).

I would like to end with a quote from Marcus Garvey (1887–1940):
A people without the knowledge of their past history, origin and culture is like a tree without roots.

Lightening the heavy burden for black children in care is well overdue.

References

Watts, F. (1984) *I am a Muslim*, Franklin Watts Ltd.

Avon and Somerset Constabulary (1998) *Faces of Britain – a cultural guide*, Avon and Somerset Constabulary.

Noss, D. and Noss, J. (1984) *A History of the World's Religions*, London: Macmillan Publishing Company.

Lebon, J. (1969) *An Introduction to Human Geography*, Hutchinson & Co. Ltd.

Sumpton, A. (1997) *The Particular Needs of Black Children* (Sec. C, Module 24, C91-97), Paramount Welfare, National Induction Training for the Guardian Service, Department of Health.

Fry, T. (Nov/Dec 1994) *Introducing the new growth standards*. In *Professional Care of Mother and Child*, 4:8, pp 231–233.

National Geographic CD-Rom (1995) *Picture Atlas of the World*, Macintosh and Windows Version, Grades 4–12, Adult.

7 Meeting the needs of transracially adopted young people

Michael Mallows

This chapter provides an update of an event that happened some years ago when I organised a trip to Wales with a group of teenagers. Despite the time gap, many of the issues raised are still relevant, perhaps even more so today. It explores the experiences of transracially placed black youngsters and their white adoptive parents and highlights important areas of consideration for practitioners and parents.

Abercrave weekend

Seven transracially adopted black adolescents, four boys and three girls, accompanied another man, two women, and myself (all experienced youth or social workers), to spend some days together at the Abercrave Centre in North Wales (Mallows, 1989).

Looking back, I still remember many of the highs and lows, the frustrations and feistiness as well as the humour and anxieties that we all shared. The kids, and indeed the adults, threw ourselves into an exhilarating and exhausting experience.

The teens demonstrated real concern for each other, in between squabbles and rows. For example, when one lad disclosed that he was terribly homesick, the other boys showed a remarkable degree of tolerance, understanding, empathy, and compassion. The whole trip was a constant fluctuation between such consideration of each other's feelings and total disregard for anyone's sensibilities. It was a very positive experience that we shared and created, and we all benefited from it.

With the amusement that distance allows, I recall the gap between my grandiose expectations of the event and the inadequacy of my skills and knowledge for achieving what I had hoped to.

Young people

Most of the youngsters were of African-Caribbean origin or of mixed parentage. I had anticipated time to discuss issues of "race" and identity in the context of transracial adoption with teenagers who were being brought up by parents of a different "race" and colour.

These young people were, without exception, in good homes with loving families. They experienced, mostly, very comfortable or high standards of living. Foreign holidays, horses, holiday homes, and good education were typical of their lifestyles. They frequently ate out with their parents. They were, after they settled down and settled in for the trip, confident, cheeky, articulate, middle-class youngsters.

Now, after 13 years of experience at the Post Adoption Centre in London, it remains the case that many transracially adopted people still find little opportunity to share feelings with other people in a similar situation.

Although the Association of Trans Racially Adopted People (ATRAP) is now in existence, it is either not easily accessible or, for a number of reasons, not appropriate for all transracial adoptees. It is also still the case that many white parents of minority ethnic adoptees feel reluctant or hesitant to talk about the issue of "race" with their children.

A considerable amount of harm is caused by the fact that these youngsters feel unable to express or are unwilling to communicate their struggle for identity. This often means that white parents may have little or no idea what their children are experiencing, or the questions they are asking. This ignorance is, of course, neither exclusive to transracial adoption, or to adoption *per se*, but the ordinary angst and antagonism of adolescence are complicated by the fact of adoption, and often further exacerbated by the racial dimension. Denial of this, though explicable, is lamentable.

The Wales weekend was rich with examples of young people being denied, albeit without malicious intent, a connection with, or an understanding of, their "race" and roots. They had all, for example, eaten in Italian, Chinese, Indian, Spanish, and even Mexican restaurants in Britain. However, not one of them had ever eaten West Indian cuisine. At first sight of a traditional West Indian meal, they were aghast; at first taste, they were delighted by the culture shock. Also, most of the youngsters on the weekend couldn't recall even talking to other *adopted* people, let alone someone transracially adopted.

Years later, I still counsel adults who maintain secrecy and silence about their adoption, with the loneliness that that ensues. For "same race" adoptees, it takes very little for adoption to remain hidden. For transracially adopted school children it can be quite difficult: PTA and parents' meetings, dental or medical check-ups, meetings with friends and neighbours mean that, in a thousand ways, transracial adoption is an "open secret". There is no reason that adoption should ever be a secret, but the adopted youngster is seldom consulted about who should know and has even less choice.

Usually coinciding with puberty, the young person begins to realise, painfully, that adoption means loss. He or she has lost the "might-have-been" of the birth family. The festivals and birthdays. When there is friction at home he or she may dream of the "if-onlys" and "what-ifs" of a life unlived. The transracial adoptee has other kinds of loss to deal with. The loss of heritage, understanding, perhaps community. As one of them said: 'Friends say it shouldn't matter, but they don't see what I see. It does matter. It's as if I can't be accepted as English by anyone, black or white!'

Social work practice

There is no doubt that social work practice has moved on from the attitude lamented by a family placement worker: 'We're still trying to get *social workers* to come to terms with life story work!' However, a great many professionals do not know how to raise, let alone address, issues about transracial adoptions with white people in a way that will be appropriate, effective, *and* make a difference.

Families are close to, or way beyond, crisis point by the time professionals get involved in post-adoption situations. Available resources seem to decrease in direct proportion to the increasing pressures on all concerned. The planning and preparation of prospective adopters, indeed much of adoption itself, seems to be based on a model of family life that was already being romanticised in the 19th century. Hand in hand with Victorian values and nonsense about bad blood, I also detect a 1960s optimism, almost a naivety at times, about peace and love. Love is seldom enough, especially now when so many children bring with them physical and emotional scars from previous families or placements. Love may get them through, but it may not heal them. There may always be something askew in their lives, indeed in their hearts.

This is evidenced by the attempt to reverse the good work done towards a "same-race" placement policy. I have worked with many transracial families. With few exceptions, the parents are decent, loving, caring, supportive people who are doing the best possible job of parenting. There is no guarantee that a transracial placement will fail – and no certainty that a "same-race" placement will work.

Some of those who adopted more than ten years ago sometimes feel frustrated by the change of attitude in terms of the racial dimension. They may feel particularly challenged by my comments. The issue, however, is not about transracial adopters, it is a much broader issue than that! I want to assist and support parents to do the best they can for their children. When I work with a transracial family, I do not see them as an adoptive family in crisis, nor as a transracial family in trouble. I see a family struggling to make sense of their struggle, and hoping I can help. I endeavour to help by explaining and exploring issues of "race", adoption, adaptive grieving, adolescence, and anything else that helps them to make sense of their family dynamics. I will, if necessary, coach parents in parenting, listening, and negotiating skills. I want to help any parents to do the best job they can as parents. I am not concerned with political expediencies or meeting targets. I am concerned with increasing parents' awareness of the underlying issues for their black, Asian or Chinese children.

Some parents find this approach acceptable, though uncomfortable. Some find it intolerable and even accuse me of "taking sides". A parent recently accused me of making things worse by pointing out what everybody knew. She demanded that I tell her what to do differently with her teenage, transracially adopted son. Then she vociferously decried any suggestion that touched on his racial identity. "Race", she declared, was not the issue; all the family problems, however, were his fault! I believe this woman and her husband, and their son, had been let down by the social workers. There had been, and there is still, little input on "race" and even less on teaching counselling or even *listening* skills for the parents.

Socio-economic pressures usually have the most detrimental impact on those who are already disadvantaged. These pressures might increase the likelihood of either biological families or potential adopters not being able to care for the children from their own community. This could increase the convenient myth that there are not enough black families willing to offer their homes and hearts to those youngsters who need them.

The racist murder of the black teenager, Stephen Lawrence, is currently raising awareness that racism, reinforced by institutionalised and organisational practices, is still underpinned by the myth of white supremacy. One way that racism severely disadvantages black people includes being "denied" permission or support for discovering and understanding roots and identity when adopted by white people. That denial may be the adoptee's internalisation of what is *not* said rather than what *is*. Parents may be sincere in expecting and encouraging some sort of appropriate contact with blood relatives. However, they may never initiate discussion about that aspect of their child's heritage.

White adoptive parents

I neither deny nor discount the extraordinary love and commitment that many white adoptive parents have made to their Asian, African, African-Caribbean, South American, Chinese, or children of other minority ethnic backgrounds. But going the extra mile may require something extra.

Some parents may choose not merely to act as advocates for their children's racial and cultural heritage. They may decide not simply to champion their children's cause in the endless fight against racism. They may also empathise with their children's pain *without feeling guilty*.

Many white adoptive parents of black children feel guilty; others are merely defensive. Either feeling may be interpreted by the child as proof that their parents are not comfortable with the "race" issue – which, of course, means with *them!* Others express *commitment* in terms of guilt and remorse. Guilt often becomes an excuse for inaction – and commitment without action is like a river without water.

A frequent and emotive question focuses, rather simplistically, on whether black children should be left to languish in residential units when there are white people willing to give them a loving home. Put that simply, of course not. The question itself is spurious, designed to tug at the heart strings and distract from the broader issues of ignorance and racism in education, in social work training, in the legal system, and in so many areas of our lives.

Professionals and politicians who pay lip service to the best interests of the child are often too busy with the next campaign, or the latest crisis, to walk the extra mile. There is an attitude based on the apparent assumption that finding a "right" white family for this black child will make everything all right.

When planning for the Abercrave weekend, many of the adoptive parents said something to the effect that their child 'didn't have a problem with the issue of transracial adoption!' Or, 'S/he doesn't like to talk about it, maybe next time.' Or, 'S/he does like to mix with brown (sic) children at school, and I don't think s/he'd get much from a weekend like that.'

At the same time, social workers and youth workers clamoured for places for 17 and 18-year-olds (only secondary school age teens were allowed) who were having problems at home, or had already left or been ejected from home acrimoniously. The professionals believed these young adults would benefit greatly from the chance to discuss issues of "race", colour, culture, and personal identity with others who shared their experience.

There is, I believe, a strong link between youngsters who "refuse" to talk about pigmentation, colour, even adoption, with their white parents, and older black adoptees who are struggling to make sense of who they are and where they belong. As one 26-year-old said to me a few weeks ago, 'I don't fit in anywhere. I never feel that I belong'.

Nancy Newton-Verrier's (1994) concept of the primal wound describes early separation from the birth mother as a traumatic, psychosomatic shock reverberating through an individual's head, heart and gut leading to a whole raft of emotional, psychological and behavioural problems. A young black person, displaced from his or her family of origin, may experience a similar blow to the psyche. If the second coin in a stack is slightly askew, all those stacked above will be out of alignment.

Assume that a child has not been abused or traumatised, and the prospective parents have been assessed as an ideal couple. Everything goes well; they are a success story. Even so, a much loved, "well adjusted", transracial adoptee will, of necessity, struggle with the obvious differences between him or herself and their adoptive parent. Let us further suppose that the parents have been very open about the child's "race" and culture. They celebrate appropriate festivals, may even take the child to visit his or her biological parents' home country. They read newspapers to keep them abreast of issues relevant to their child's origins in case he or she ever wants to know. They engage in ongoing debate to ensure that friends are aware of the issues and implications. They freely discuss their own struggles and confusions with their child. Ideal.

Their child, however, is going through changes: adaptive grieving, puberty, independence, identity. Struggles to develop a sense of self – which usually, at this stage, means some form of rebelliousness: 'I am not YOU, I am myself! But who am I?' The issue of "race" is revisited, 'I am not white! *You* are not black. I don't want to be different. We are not the same.'

To quote another recent 20-year-old client, 'I had almost no positive images at home. I wasn't given an opportunity to see how black people operate. If I asked my parents they didn't know, and they didn't try to find out. I knew they didn't want *me* to talk about it.'

A child's reluctance to talk about colour, "race" or transracial adoption, is often an indication of the child's knowledge or suspicion that parents, or other adults, will not know how to respond. Many transracial adoptees, be they young teenagers or middle aged, find it impossible to share their true feelings with their parents. They cannot, *dare* not, reveal their hurt for fear of causing pain to their parents. Others fear their parents won't be supportive, or the level of mutual anger is so intense that nothing but sparks or silence pass between them.

I consider it the adoptive parents' responsibility to keep the issue of "race" and identity alive for their children. Parents who feel accused or blamed by this tend to be those who have done least to acknowledge, let alone celebrate, their children's difference and uniqueness. This failure can deprive children of a foundation for racial pride later in life, and could deprive parents of their children's trust and confidence in this vital area. Adoptive parents who refuse to discuss "blackness", or claim they are "colour blind", even refusing to "see" colour, are denying their child in a profound way. Even worse, if they also have biological children, they may claim to treat adoptive and biological children the same. This often implies, even if it is not intended and if only to the children, treating the black children as if they are white! Youngsters who are ethnically visible (i.e. people whose pigmentation is *visibly* different from the majority) have particular needs in our society. There are additional nuances for the transracially adopted and their families.

Professionals and parents must ensure that these issues are not swept aside by a tide of liberal ignorance. More resources must be invested in race awareness and anti-racism work targeted specifically at prospective adopters. This training should focus on increasing awareness of the racist implications of casual comments and everyday language. It could help people to recognise that racist attitudes, although neither overt nor conscious, are endemic in our culture.

Awareness is just a first step, though. And, in some of the preparation for prospective adopters, even that first step is tentative and timid. I would question any "race" training that was conducted solely by white people, and further question any training that failed to challenge assumptions and complacency. Challenge via caring confrontation is the second step. This requires debate that sheds light, rather than argument that generates nothing but heat. Third and subsequent steps would require that people commit not only to learning and understanding, but also to *doing* something, taking action that will make a manifest difference.

The dance
Advertising, recruiting, and retaining would-be adopters is expensive; losing them is costly. **'Choreographing the Dance'** is a workshop for professionals who match children with adoptive parents and foster carers. Family placement workers who attend these workshops inform me that they are reluctant to be too demanding or challenging during assessments for fear of alienating applicants. Many decisions are based on politics and practicalities. A non-assertive stance can create a collusive dynamic,

a dance based on professionals' requirements and applicants' anxieties. This bodes ill for the family dynamic.

Contact with hundreds of transracially adoptive families over the last 13 years suggests that many transracial adoptees still experience a form of racism at home ('I don't see colour!') stemming from this lack of appropriate challenge to *and education for* prospective adopters.

Adoptees can interpret this, if not as actual racism, at least as a tacit support for an inherently racist society. They may perceive it as a lack of support for the community with which they may one day identify.

This perception can be reinforced by the argument that the adoptive family is the child's community. Whatever validity there may be in that argument, it is wise to assume that he or she will, in time, come to wonder, to question, to seek information about his or her racial and cultural origins. Better to assume that he or she will begin to make connections with, may meet or have relationships with people from a community where the skin colour "fits".

Given that everything we do for children helps or hinders the "adult in the making", training adopters to work with young black people needs to commence, by example and by expectation, *during* the assessment.

References

Mallows, M. (1989) 'Abercrave weekend: exploring the needs of transracially adopted young people'. In *Adoption and Fostering*, 13:3.

Verrier, N. (1994) *The Primal Wound*, Baltimore: Gateway Press Inc.

8 Educational needs of black children in care

Toyin Okitikpi

Introduction

There is a dearth of information on the educational achievements of black children who are being looked after in the care system. More importantly, there is very little discussion about how the educational needs of black children can best be met whilst they are still in care to help raise their level of educational attainment. Although there are a number of publications which have attempted to address the general area of black children in education (Stone, 1981; Verma and Bagley, 1984; Milner, 1983) there is very little published work which offers ideas and techniques that workers and carers can use with a black child in care. This chapter explores some of the ideas which are currently being used by parents and carers who have very little or no involvement with social services, and considers whether such ideas can also be used for black children looked after in public care.

The ideas to be discussed cover areas such as:

- Closer partnership between teachers and social workers (including carers and care workers)
- Setting homework
- Worker/carer's involvement with homework
- Sports
- Supplementary schools
- Religion
- Extracurricular activities

I would suggest that these areas could prove to be very helpful to the general development of a black child in care. They can provide a base from which the child can be enabled to build a more solid future. Although these ideas and suggestions are well known and very familiar to many workers, carers and parents, nevertheless they have seldom been considered or used consciously to form part of an overall long-term plan for black children in care.

The importance of formal education

It is worth noting that the 1989 Children Act recognises the importance of education for all children, irrespective of their social and cultural background. As a way of making it clear that this is viewed very seriously, the Act deals with this aspect specifically. In Part 1 Section 1 (subsection 3b) the court is asked to have particular regard to a child's 'physical, emotional and educational needs'. Section 36 subsections 1, 3 and 4 confirm that the court has the power to impose an order should it feel that the child is of school age and is 'not being properly educated'.

The underlying ethos of this section of the Act is that all children, irrespective of their abilities and capabilities, are entitled to some sort of education. To comply with the Act the onus is on those who are charged with the duty and the responsibility of caring for the children to ensure that their educational needs are considered seriously and that steps are taken to ensure school attendance.

The importance of education as a vehicle for personal, emotional, intellectual and professional development should not be underestimated nor should it be taken for granted. Education can potentially be both liberating and oppressive (Freire, 1970). As Cooper (1994) observed, education can be a means by which people who have been subjugated and "excluded" change their ascribed role for a place as a full participating member in the historical process. Similarly, but less poetically perhaps, Brittan and Maynard (1984) highlighted the often perceived potential of education when they asserted that education is often treated as an extension of primary socialisation, in that it provides both formal and informal training outside the private confines of family life. They continued:

> In addition, it is also proclaimed as a potential "leveller" in its supposed promotion of equality of opportunity and disregard of social difference. (Brittan and Maynard, 1984:53)

However, they also went on to demolish the premise on which the proclamation rests, by exposing how the education system can also be the vehicle by which racist and sexist doctrines are perpetuated. Nevertheless, Brittan and Maynard (1984) like many other authors (such as Verma and Bagley, 1975; Blyth and Milner, 1997) are very astute in noting the intrinsic value of education. They acknowledge, both implicitly and explicitly, that despite its shortcomings and in spite of its ramifications, it is through education that liberation, empowerment and self-determination are able to have any real meaning. Pitts (1998) suggested that education can be emancipatory because it has the capacity to effect positive change and to enable the possibility of transforming negative and wounding prior experiences into intellectual and emotional resources.

Poor expectations
In a study by the Social Services Inspectorate (SSI) and the Office for Standards in Education (OFSTED) (1995) into the education of children in care, it was found that many of the 45,000 school children in care missed school regularly and few of them gained academic or vocational qualifications. Overall the inspection found that:
- the educational standards attained by these children were too low;
- in general social workers, teachers and children's carers gave insufficient priority to educational progress and levels of achievement;
- liaison between social workers, teachers and those caring for children was frequently unsatisfactory and therefore the approach taken to raising educational achievement lacked co-ordination;
- parents or other adults with parental responsibility for the children were not sufficiently informed about nor did they sufficiently engage with their educational progress;
- educational progress was damaged by drift and delay in implementing decisions about care placements;
- insufficient information and training for social workers, teachers and carers contributed to a lack of concerted action to raise standards.

These were the main findings of the report into the education of children looked after by local authorities. Although the report did not distinguish between the racial or ethnic origins of the children, it is safe to assume that, amongst the numbers quoted in the study, a sizeable proportion of them would have been black. But, because there are an insufficient number of local authorities gathering data on the actual numbers of black children in their care, it is impossible to know the extent to which black children lack proper schooling during their period in care. Similarly, there is no information about what happens to these children, educationally, whilst they are in care and, more importantly, their qualification attainments beyond the age of 16. There is, for example, no central information kept of the children's general progress as they grow up, no records kept of their educational achievements in terms of how many GCSEs or A Levels they have obtained or how many go on to universities or colleges of further and higher education.

A report by the Who Cares? Trust (1997) revealed the extent to which children in care have a different educational experience to children who were not subject to social services intervention. The report estimated that between 12 and 19 per cent of the former go on to further education, compared with 68 per cent of the general population. The report further highlighted and to a large extent reinforced the SSI and OFSTED findings about the plight of children in care and the poor consideration given to their schooling. According to the Who Cares? Trust's report, up to 75 per cent of children in local authority care left school with no formal qualifications. As the joint SSI/OFSTED report revealed;

> Underachievement was more severe in the secondary school than in primary school. The children in secondary schools seldom reached standards close to those expected. The majority did not reach standards commensurate with their ability. (SSI/OFSTED, 1995:11)

What is being argued in this chapter is that there is a need for workers and carers to be more aware of the importance of education for all children being looked after, both in the formal sense as well as informally. Barbara Fletcher (1997) author of the report, *Who Cares about Education?,* found that in general social workers and the children's school did not share information and that there was a lack of effective planning about the ongoing educational needs of the children, and those responsible for their day-to-day care did not seem to value education highly enough. Her findings, which are not dissimilar to earlier findings by Fletcher-Campbell and Hall (1990) revealed that the children experienced unnecessary moves of school or were out of school for prolonged periods. Firth (1995) also found that children in local authority care were at greater risk of permanent exclusion from school. Part of the explanation is that schools, social workers and carers have no or lower expectations of looked after children and this can contribute to underachievement, poor attainment and failure.

An article in *The Times* (10 April 1995) perhaps best illustrates the lack of encouragement children in care receive with regard to their schooling. In the article two teenagers, both white, female and 16 years of age, conveyed their sense of frustration about the lack of support from the adults around them. In one case the girl was moved to five different schools over a six-year period. She said, 'I was never brilliant at school but sometimes I tried quite hard. I wanted to go to university but I didn't know anyone from care who had done that.' Most tellingly she said, 'Teachers aren't interested if you don't have a real parent demanding results'.

In another example reported to the Who Cares? Trust researchers, a 14-year-old is said to have complained that, "Everybody, including teachers, treats you like an idiot because you are in care. They presume you are bad'. (*The Guardian*, 18 December 1994)

Another young person explained, 'Before I went into care, I was in the top sets and everything. They put me in the bottom sets as soon as I moved into care and moved schools'. (*The Guardian*, 18 December 1994)

I believe that these particular adolescents are not necessarily angry with an individual teacher who may or may not have paid them any attention, although their disappointments, dissatisfaction and frustrations are clear enough, but the sadness is about the lack of a "third force" i.e. a social worker, carer or key-worker who has the child's general interests at heart and who is concerned about her long-term future and about her total education. Although the examples mentioned are of white adolescents, one can extrapolate from their experiences that there would be countless numbers of voiceless black children whose stories have not been heard but who share similar frustrations. For many black children the general lack of support and encouragement they experience is further compounded by an educational system that appears too eager to disrupt their schooling through short periods of exclusion and in some cases permanently expelling them. Pat Verity of the National Foster Care Association (NFCA) picked up this point in her letter to *The Guardian* (April 1998) when she referred to the 'explosion in school exclusion'. In it she noted that 25 per cent of youngsters aged 14–16 in public care were either excluded or not attending school regularly; according to her they were also '10 times more likely than their peers to be permanently excluded'. Her findings dovetail with the Commission for Racial Equality (CRE) and The Children Society's research (1997) which found that, in general, African-Caribbean children were more likely to be excluded or expelled from school than their white peers. For many black children in care this aspect of their experience is often missed or ignored because other issues are regarded as more pressing.

Education and the black child
It is worthwhile to remember that one should be careful about evoking stereotypical utterances to use as an exemplar of a particular view, but in this case there is merit in workers and carers taking note of the underlying message behind the well known "adage" that black parents in general have high educational aspirations for their children (Stone, 1981; Cronin, 1984; Mason, 1995). These parental ideals have often been an area of contention between some teachers and black parents. Teachers point out that there are often discrepancies between what a black parent feels their child ought to be able to achieve and what the teachers feel they know about what the child is capable of achieving (Stone, 1981). It is this area of discrepancy where the battle lines of differences are drawn. It is also this area of discrepancy that is renamed by many black parents as racial discrimination on the part of the white teachers against their children. The outcome of this means that there is mistrust of the educational system in general and, more often than not, the parent also loses faith in the school that their child attends. Furthermore, many express concerns about a school ethos that appears to be based on a view that children left undirected and un-pressured will find their own balance. The lack of understanding of the educational aims of the school, the setting of poor standards, low or poor levels of discipline together with the lack of trust as to the motives that underpin the school's

approach towards the black child, culminate in very little respect for the school in general and the teachers in particular, whom black parents regard and sometimes experience as people that are instrumental in reinforcing discriminatory and prejudicial practices.

Black parents have for many years voiced their unhappiness about the lack of opportunities for black children within the education system. They have expressed the opinion that teachers have low expectations and there is little encouragement for the children to pursue vocational, professional or academic career patterns. Milner (1983), Stone (1981) and the CRE (1997), have all, to different degrees, highlighted the extent to which black children have been badly served by the state education system. The combination of racial discrimination, in this case the belief that black children are incapable of any educational achievement in school apart from displaying sporting prowess, and the old "class war", that is, black working class parents feeling unable to engage with the school system, either because they had gone through a very different educational system or as a result of their own, perhaps, negative experience of school, all impact on the black child as he or she attempts to meander through the complex process of being able to read, write and do arithmetic.

There is ample evidence to support the finding that black children are failing within the state educational system (Troyna, 1986; Gill, Mayor and Blair, 1991), although increasingly, many studies tend to make a distinction between children from African-Caribbean, African and Southern Asian backgrounds and their educational achievements (Mason, 1995; Troyna and Carrington, 1990). These studies concluded that although in general black children experience a great deal of disadvantage, when given the opportunity and parental backing they tend to do very well in school and general exam results are better (particularly for children of Indian origin) than for white children of the same age. Mason's findings are worth repeating here as they set out very clearly both the contradictions and discrepancies that exist with regard to children of minority ethnic groups. As Mason highlighted,

... when the focus turns to those aged between 16 and 24 who are no longer in full-time education, the pattern which emerges is somewhat different. Here the LFS (Labour Force Survey, 1990) data suggest that

among both men and women, those of African, Asian and Indian origin are better qualified than white people. Although the evidence continues to suggest that Afro-Caribbean men are less qualified than white men (levels of qualification for women in these groups are comparable with one another). (Jones, 1993 cited Mason, 1995:66)

There is little doubt that, in general, the overwhelming indicators are that many black children (black boys in particular) leave school with little or poor educational results that would enable them to enhance their career options. There is no suggestion here that a black child gaining qualifications would be immune from racial discrimination or prejudices, but merely that academic results and professional qualifications make a difference in increasing opportunities in the career market place.

With our knowledge of education as a potentially positive and important contributor to individual development, it is somewhat surprising that very little attention is paid to ensure that black children in care are encouraged to stay on longer at school to gain some, or better qualifications, or that every effort is not made to ensure that he or she has access to the sort of educational support which would have been hoped for and considered important had they stayed with their family.

As a general rule in social work there is a great deal of emphasis on the physical, emotional and psychological development of the black child. There are, quite rightly, questions asked about how to help the child develop a sense of self with a positive racial identity and self-image. Indeed, some of these ideas are explored elsewhere in this publication. A number of publications have contributed to our understanding of the psychological, emotional and physical development of the black child and the importance of early childhood experiences (Wilson, 1978; Ahmed *et al*, 1986; ABSWAP, 1983; Barn, 1993). This theme of the social and psychological development of the black child is very important and worth further consideration. For example, Barn (1994) argues that:

. . . a child separated from his/her family, friends and relatives is at a great risk of losing contact with their racial and cultural community. S/he is likely to experience feelings of isolation, alienation and insecurity. When issues of race and ethnicity are added to this, the

situation becomes even more complex. So a child's enquiries about Who am I? Where am I? Why am I here? And what is going to happen to me? will need to be handled carefully, sensitively and addressed in the interests of the child. (Barn, 1994:3)

These questions, which I describe as "primary tasks", are important because they help to focus on the feelings and experiences being worked through by a child growing up in care. The pursuance of answers can, of course, be a lifelong quest, since children (as well as adults) who have not been in care are also working through and trying to answer the same kind of questions (Erikson, 1959). Although there is some merit in acknowledging this point, nevertheless there is still a need to recognise the painful emotional turmoil involved in being received into care with all the destabilising effects and the uncertainties it involves.

Bearing this in mind, there is a need to seriously consider these "primary tasks" (Who am I/Where do I belong?) alongside the more long-term questions of what happens to black children once they leave the general protective cocoon of the social care system. Questions such as: What are the possible options available to them? What are their chances of surviving the harsh reality of independence? How is a black child who has spent the most formative part of his/her life in care going to maximise and realise their full potential if, when they eventually leave care, they are unable to read or write adequately? An answer in the negative to the questions above will have an impact on the black child's ability to compete with other children, both black and white, who may not have been in care but have had the same or a similar level of disadvantage.

There is a glimpse of the possible future that awaits some black children who have gone through the care system. In a survey on homelessness conducted by Centrepoint in the early 1990s, it was highlighted that there was a noticeable increase in the number of black youngsters sleeping rough on the streets of London. It was acknowledged that, as with their white counterparts, the vast majority of these young black children had been in the care of a local authority.

Pat Verity of the NFCA made a similar point but mentioned that compared to their peers the children were more likely to be unemployed between the ages of 16 and 24, 60 times more likely to join the ranks of the young homeless and 50 times more likely to serve time in prison. (*The Guardian*, 3 April 1998).

It is ironic that having being looked after by the local authority because it was deemed necessary perhaps as a result of parental neglect or estrangement that, on leaving care, black children should end up on the homeless, jobless and illiterate statistics lists.

As has already been mentioned, Section 36 of the Children Act 1989 makes it a clear expectation that children of school age should be properly educated. This needs to be taken more seriously than it has been to date. In general, despite its limitations and its scant regard for the needs of children from minority ethnic communities, the spirit of the Children Act 1989 can provide the basic foundation upon which workers and carers can build. As the Act states, a child's race, culture, ethnicity, religious and educational needs must be taken into consideration.

Making a difference

Workers and carers need to maintain a healthy scepticism about any publication which proclaims to be able to offer 'an already prepared solution' to what appears to be a difficult and complex set of problems. However, workers and carers are urged to consider all new and old ideas for their usefulness before they discard or discredit them. Whilst originality of ideas is not being claimed in this instance, it is not common for all these ideas to be given due regard in such a focused way for children who are so disadvantaged. In essence there is nothing new in the ideas mentioned below because many parents and carers who have no involvement with social work or social services make use of them in varying forms. Indeed, so do many workers involved with children in care. For there to be a major change in the experience of black children in the care system, as well as placing emphasis on workers going through antidiscriminatory practice processes they also need to take a number of practical measures to help black children prepare for life after leaving care. Workers need to look at forging a closer link with the child's school; Spencer (1982) found that one of the explanations for the academic successes of black girls was the support they got from their mothers with homework. I would therefore suggest that a much closer attention needs to be placed on not just setting homework but for those involved in the day-to-day care of children being more active in supporting the black child. The role of sport in children's lives needs to be reconsidered and supplementary schools may also be able to provide a much needed additional help and support for black children experiencing difficulties in mainstream school. The positive contribution that religion can make in a child's life is also often underplayed. Finally, there are a range of suggestions under extracurricular activities that black children being looked after can be encouraged to be involved in as part of their overall development. It is possible to reverse and minimise the cycle of disadvantage that black children being looked after experience. Each of these ideas cannot be considered in isolation but need to be considered as part of a wider strategy of transformation.

Closer partnership between teacher and carer/social worker

The National Curriculum, which underpins every aspects of a child's school life, recognises the need for co-operation between home and school. This idea is of course not new in education – the Plowden Report (1967), a now much maligned document, highlighted the importance of the school–home relationship, and the need for closer partnership with social services. Douglas (1967) explored in depth the crucial role that the linkage plays in the educational development of children.

The Education Reform Act 1990 and the Children Act 1989 have picked up and to some extent developed some of the points made in earlier legislation. Also importantly, they all acknowledge, in their different ways, the importance of the triad – the child, parent/carer and teacher – and the need for a closer working relationship between them.

If a child were not in care a teacher would know immediately who to contact if there were problems regarding the child's school work or concern about their general behaviour. The difficulty with a child in care is that the teacher may not have any contact person for the child. In other words, there is not always a face or a name to consistently associate with the child. The child's carer/worker needs to make themselves known to the teacher to initiate the two-way process that will support the child in school. The teacher then knows who to address, the child knows who to turn to with homework, help or problems in school, and the carer/

worker has established personal contact with the one person closest to the child in school. Often it is the school which initiates contact with the child's social worker and it is invariably due to a problem arising in school – the school rarely has contact with anyone other than the field social worker. The worker/carer needs to be in contact with the school, if possible, attending open evenings, concerts, etc.

Setting of homework
Statements from Tony Blair about homework prior to his election victory found support in many quarters across the political spectrum. Without doubt, in my view, there is great value in children being set homework. The experience of many teachers is that it gives many children who perhaps have not been able to get the individual attention of the teacher in the classroom, the chance to get support from their worker/carer on a one off or ongoing project. This allows the child to review the work currently in hand as well as learn the skill of gathering information and using the wealth of natural knowledge i.e. the generally untapped resources of people around them. It also provides children with an opportunity to think about subjects outside the usual forum, and it begins to teach them the benefits of exploring subjects and working independently. The assumption is often that children "in care" have other worries on their minds and that doing homework is of least importance as there are other more important aspects in the child's life to think about. There is no doubt that the child's physical, psychological and emotional well-being are important and one would be hard pressed to justify the negligence of these basic needs. But, as has often been agreed by many professionals, the yardstick by which "good enough" parenting is assessed does not exclude the need to ensure that the child's educational requirements are given serious consideration. Most schools have homework policies but they are only successful with the co-operation of the adults involved with the child out of school.

Worker/carer's involvement with homework
Another reason for considering homework is that it firmly locks the teacher and the black child's carer together. It is another way of forging a closer link between home and school. However, it is important to bear

in mind that although setting homework is important, not just for the academic development of the child but also to give the child a chance to perhaps catch up if they are behind with the basics, perhaps more crucially, homework can help the worker/carer to get closer to the child; it can aid communication and it is a private arena that is shared between the child and the worker/carer. It is also, of course, a place where learning is done. The reason for encouraging homework with the involvement of the carer/worker in this instance as an idea has a practical purpose. The view here is that it is not enough for workers/carers to only give the child the verbal encouragement to "go off and do" their homework; the expectation is that the worker/carer has an active role to play in this. Their role/task involves finding out whether the child has been set homework; preparing a conducive environment to enable homework to be done; and sitting down and offering advice, suggestions and learning alongside the child. Even if the worker/carer feels unable to help with the subject being studied (a tutor may prove better in some instances), the actual process of showing concern may prove just as encouraging.

The pay off is both quantifiable and unquantifiable. Quantifiable in so far as there would hopefully be an improvement in the child's knowledge and understanding about the different subject areas. This, in turn, might mean because they are able to keep up with the rest of the class, the child will have fewer reasons to miss school or disrupt lessons when they are in school. It is also unquantifiable because the emotional and psychological development of the child might be greatly improved as a result and there is also the chance of a new-found confidence as he or she finds him or herself less alienated from the more structured, formal school setting. The process of helping and working alongside the child can also foster a closer relationship between the child and their worker/carer. This gives the black child a very strong demonstrable signal that their overall well-being is important enough for a worker/carer to spend time with them.

Sports
This is a controversial area in so far as there is a history of black children (particularly African-Caribbean children) being pushed into this career path rather than other professions. The works of Mac an Ghaill (1992),

Gillborn (1990), Troyna and Carrington (1990), and Wright (1992 and 1987) provide a substantial body of evidence to support the beliefs of black parents that many white teachers see black children as athletes rather than potential intellectuals. The encouragement of black children to participate in sport does not mean that they ignore their academic studies. It is also worth noting that not all black children are going to end up as intellectuals and academics as exemplified by notable figures such as Paul Gilroy, Stuart Hall, Tariq Modood or Shama Ahmed. Some of them may indeed end up being an Ian Wright, Linford Christie, Nasser Hussain or Prince Hameed. In my view, black children should not be discouraged from actively participating in all areas of sport, but rather, school career advisers, teachers, carers and workers should inform them of the range of careers available and continuously reinforce the need to widen their options at every opportunity possible. Sport for enjoyment is positive. It encourages competition and co-operation which are both useful for the adult world and work. It can be a caring and sharing pastime that also encourages comradeship as well as acts as an important social and community connector.

Supplementary schools
There is a need for workers and carers of black children to have awareness of the range of supplementary educational provisions (Saturday or evening schools) available within the locality where the child is residing. These schools are used by many black parents as a buttress to the state education system. These schools provide both a social meeting place and an educational environment for the children. The general approach of the schools and the atmosphere which is generated, on the whole by the children themselves, makes them different from the formal school setting. Supplementary schools at best can help to boost a child's sense of confidence, both in terms of academic capability and learning to form social relationships. Some supplementary schools see it as their role to also provide the children with a positive sense of "self". A great deal of emphasis is placed on providing positive images, role learning, as well as offering opportunities for the children to learn about black history, an area of study which is not included in the National Curriculum and is often ignored by some mainstream schools.

In her book, *The Education of the Black Child in Britain*, Maureen Stone captured the essence of why many black parents turned to supplementary schools and Saturday schools to compensate for the inadequacies of and their lack of trust in the state system. She states:

'. . . *while schools try to compensate children by offering black studies and steel bands, black parents and community groups are organising Saturday schools to supplement the second-rate education which the school system offers their children.'* (Stone, 1981:11)

Religion

Although consideration of a child's religious background is enshrined within the Children Act, there is very little encouragement for black children to explore the positive aspects of their religious background. The black child's participation in the social life of their religion is as important as his or her involvement in festivals and celebrations in which they are often encouraged to participate. There is an acknowledgement and a recognition that, in the general population, there is a higher percentage of black people who are actively involved with their religious communities; however, there is little evidence to suggest that black children being looked after enjoy the same opportunity for this as adults in the community. In essence, it is not about the sensibilities of the carers/workers' own views about the merits of the various religious affiliations of the child, but a recognition that, for some black children, their involvement with a religious community could provide the stability, continuity and boundaries they need. This is especially so for a black child whose life has been characterised by a great deal of instability, movements and uncertainties (Patel, Naik and Humphries, 1997). Again, the Children Act 1989 allows for this in that it states under Section 22(5)(c) that it expects social services 'to give due consideration to the child's religious persuasion, racial origin and cultural and linguistic background'. The irony of this is that workers/carers make a great deal of effort to accommodate some children's religious beliefs, as Barn (1993) found in her study, but as a general rule it is often the case that workers/carers' personal ambiguities about religion as a whole generally influence their lack of encouragement of black children to explore the possible positive role that religion can play in their lives.

Extracurricular activities

For many children in the care system there are a number of activities which they invariably lose out on. These extracurricular activities have a role to play in the general development of the child. Encouraging the black child to join local groups such as youth clubs, Sunday school, mother tongue classes, and schemes like the Duke of Edinburgh Award Scheme can be positive influences in the child's life. Before looking at the criticisms that might be levelled at this suggestion, I think it is worthwhile to consider its beneficial aspects. These out of school activities are, for many children, a positive early learning arena. It would be uncontroversial to suggest that many workers/carers would have some awareness or at least some understanding of the benefits that these out of school organisations can provide for children in general and for black children in particular. Indeed, many black parents use these organisations and, in some cases, actively participate by offering general support and "a helping hand" during the organising of events and trips out.

These organisations can be useful in providing the black child with the opportunity to explore an inner self which is both "private and public". It increases the child's network and social contacts; it enables children to find out about themselves and also to begin to learn about their own strengths and how to extend their capabilities; it fosters independence; and it encourages children to learn what it means to share and think about others outside their immediate circle.

The sorts of activities that children are encouraged to pursue give each child the possibility of widening their general knowledge base and teaching them about socially acceptable behaviour patterns. It encourages the child to develop personal interests and friendship groups. Children are helped through the process of taking on responsibilities and about making choices. All this is done through actively working with the child towards a "self-defined goal". There are many positive by-products to a child being encouraged to be more active outside the confines of their "normal" lives, one of which is that an accumulation of all these different experiences may provide the child with moral guidance and a different exposure from that of their, perhaps, usual negative or abusive environment.

To be able to change a culture of underachievement, low expectations and social exclusion, those involved in the lives of black children in care have to look at the "total needs" of the children. Whilst the ideas offered above could lead to a nightmare scenario in which a child is ferried from one activity to another with very little thought about its benefit and appropriateness, many of the positives outweigh the negatives. Being in care is a positive option for some black children and their long-term future should not be jeopardised as a result. Currently when conferences and reviews and planning meetings are considering where a black child should be placed or what provisions would be most appropriate, there is little evidence that the child's educational requirements are given the same priority as other areas. Indeed, the SSI/OFSTED report noted that,

Many (children) face sudden changes, often without planning and preparation, which have an effect on the continuity of their learning as well as on their relationships and friendships.

(SSI/OFSTED, 1995:3)

Taking the SSI/OFSTED findings and incorporating some of the ideas presented in this chapter would have a profound effect on assessment, planning, and placement and on the implementation of care plans for the children. It would also affect how direct work with the black child is conducted, because it would require those working with and involved with the child to take a more active role. They would need to develop a heightened sense of awareness of their involvement in the child's life, an understanding of the negative experiences the black child faces, and the longer-term social realities of the black child, especially black boys.

Conclusion

In conclusion, the argument for education has already been made and accepted, similarly the importance of parental/carer support, regular school attendance, completion of homework and involvement in the wider life of the school (THES, 1998). What is being suggested here is not new nor the prerogative of only middle class children. For many years, black children who have not been in care have had access to these provisions and more. With parental/carer encouragement and support (emotional and practical) even the most difficult child can find a "place" amongst all these possibilities which would give them the opportunity to exercise a greater degree of choice.

Surely in an age in which the terms empowerment, enabling, facilitation, self-determination and partnership have entered the discourse of social work, it is important that black children in the care system are given a good educational base upon which to build their future once they leave care. However, it seems that the notions of self-determination, empowerment and partnership are used as softening words, because in reality what is wanted is a reliant, powerless client group which continues to look to social services for help, guidance and support. This, I know, could be regarded as grossly unfair. But there is something to be said for ensuring that the process to which I have referred (strengthening the black child's sense of identity and self esteem) would have a greater significance if, alongside these concepts, black children are also given the opportunity to compete effectively in a post-industrial Britain. In many respects Britain is one of the countries at the forefront of the information, technology and communication age, and in today's global economy there is a need for a multi-skilled, mobile and to some extent highly educated workforce. Black children in care should not be excluded from participating in this or be further discriminated against by dint of having spent part of their lives in the care system.

Failure to take seriously the long-term future needs of black children in care would result in a group of children who have no stake in the country or in the community, who are disconnected from mainstream society, and are alienated and estranged not just from their families but also from any sphere of positive influences. Lack of education or poor attainment levels could also mean, for many black children, lack of equal opportunities in the longer term. As the SSI/OFSTED report rightly opined,

> *Educational qualification and achievement are of paramount importance to these children if they are to lead fulfilled adult lives.*

(SSI/OFSTED, 1995:3)

To this I would add that for black children in care it is imperative that their education needs are given the highest priority.

References

Ahmed, S., Cheetham, J. and Small, J. (1986) *Social Work with Black Children and their Families*, London: BAAF/Batsford.

Arnold, R. (1997) *Raising Levels of Achievement in Boys*, National Foundation for Education Research.

Barn, R. (1993) *Black Children In The Public Care System*, London: BAAF/Batsford.

Barn, R. (1994) *Direct Work with Black Children*, an unpublished report.

Berrington, L. (1995) *The Times*, 10 April.

Blyth, E. and Milner, J. (1997) *Social Work with Children: The educational perspective*, London: Longman.

Brittan, A. and Maynard, M. (1984) *Sexism, Racism and Oppression*, London: Blackwell.

Cheetham, J. and James, W. *et al* (1981) (eds) *Social and Community Work in a Multiracial Society*, New York: Harper and Row.

Cooper, A. (1994) 'The politics of exclusion'. In *Social Work in Europe*, 1:3, pp 29–30.

Commission for Racial Equality (1997) *Exclusion from School and Racial Equality*, Osler A, CRE.

Croft, Cronin, A (1984) 'Supplementary Schools: Their role in culture maintenance, identity and underachievement'. In *New Community* X1 (3) Spring, pp 256–268.

Douglas, J. W. B. (1967) *The Home and the School*, Panther.

DoH and OFSTED (1995) *The Education of Children who are Looked After by Local Authorities*, London: HMSO.

Education Reform Act 1990, London: HMSO.

Firth, H. (1995) *Children First: A framework for action*, Hampshire County Council.

Fletcher, B. (1993) *Not Just a Name: The views of young people in foster and residential care*, London: Who Cares about Education? National Consumer Council and Who Cares? Trust.

Fletcher-Campbell, F. and Hall, C. (1990) *Changing Schools? Changing People? The education of children in care*, National Foundation for Education Research.

Freire, P. (1970) *Cultural Actions for Freedom*, Penguin Books.

Gill, D., Mayor, B. and Blair, M. (1992) *Racism and Education Structure and Strategies*, Sage.

Gill, D., Mayor, B. and Blair, M. (eds) (1999) 'Students' Schooling Experience'. In *Racism and Education: Structures and strategies*, Sage.

Gillborn, D. (1990) *'Race' Ethnicity and Education*, Unwin Hyman.

Mac an Ghaill, M. (1988) *Young, Gifted and Black: Student–teacher relations in the schooling of black youth*, Oxford: Oxford University Press.

Mac an Ghaill, M. (1992) *Coming of Age in 1980s England: Reconceptualising black students' schooling experience.* In Gill, D., Mayor, B. and Blain, M. *Racism and Education Structures and Strategies*, Sage.

Mason, D. (1995) *Race and Ethnicity in Modern Britain*, Oxford: Oxford University Press.

Milner, D. (1983) *Children and Race: Ten years on*, Ward Lock Educational.

Patel, N., Naik, D. and Humphries, B. (eds) (1997) *Visions of Reality: Religion and ethnicity in social work*, Sage.

Pitts, J. (1998) *Education as Personal Liberation*, Russell House.

Plowden, B. (1967) *Children and their Primary Schools*, London: HMSO.

Spencer, D. (1982) 'Staying on helps blacks to exam success'. In *Times Education Supplement*, 8 October.

Stone, M. (1981) *The Education of the Black Child in Britain: Myth of multiracial school*, Fontana.

The Children Act 1989, London: HMSO.

The Eggleston Report (1986) *Education for some: A summary of the Eggleston Report on the education and vocational experiences of young black people*, Runnymede Research Report, London: Runnymede Trust.

The Guardian, 'The lost boys and girls', 18 December 1994.

The Guardian, 'Lessons of exclusion', 3 April 1998.

THES, 10 April 1998.

Tomlinson, S. (1980) 'Ethnic minority parents & education'. In Craft, M., Raynor, J. and Cohen, L. (eds) *Linking Home and School*, 3rd edn, New York: Harper and Row Publishers.

Troyna, B. and Carrington (1990) *Education Racism and Reform*, London: Routledge.

Troyna, B. (1986) *Racism, Education and the State*, Croom Helm.

Verma, G. K. and Bagley, C. (1975) *Race and Education Across Cultures*, Heinemann Educational Books.

Verma, G. K. and Bagley, C. (1984) *Race Relations and Cultural Differences*, St Martins Press.

Wilson, A. N. (1978) *The Developmental Psychology of the Black Child*, Africana.

Wright, C. (1992) *Race Relations in the Primary School*, Fulton.

Wright, C. (1987) *Black 1997 Students – White Teachers* in Troyna, B. (ed) *Racial Inequality in Education*, Tavistock.

9 A black adoptive parent's perspective

Sally Baffour

Introduction

In the light of the many complexities that surround work with black children, the first question that comes to mind on the subject is, 'How do you do it?' How do you help a black child, in the care system in Britain, develop a positive sense of identity that will enable him or her to grow up just like any other white or black child living at home with their birth parents anywhere in the world?

There is no one single formula and the fact that I am a black woman does not make me an expert either. What my husband and I (in particular) have done as parents has been, like any other parent, through trial and error and mainly drawing on my experience as a child growing up in Ghana.

My background

My origins

I was born and educated up to Secondary School level in Ghana and came at the age of 17 to study Interior Design in England, quite by chance because the course was not offered in any of the universities in Ghana. I am from a very large and close-knit family of 18 brothers and sisters and an even larger extended family who have been very supportive and as such I have had a very stable background.

My parents

My father, an educationalist, believed in children. My mother, a house-wife and seamstress, also shares the same belief. Throughout my child-hood, several children were educated by my father and some stayed with us occasionally.

My husband's background
His early school life in Britain

My husband Tetteh, also Ghanaian-born, lived in Ghana up to the age of six. Due to his father's job as a roving diplomat, youngest son Tetteh and his siblings were sent to private schools in England where he boarded from the age of 6 to 17 years in the 1960s. He was one of the very few black pupils in the two boarding schools he went to. With this background, Tetteh's outlook on life, although fundamentally similar to mine, is from a different angle.

Rediscovering Ghana

Tetteh discovered the rich culture of different rites of passage for the different sexes from birth through to death. He soon began to appreciate the various enriching traditions still practised in the system side by side with Christianity, in spite of Christianity's failed attempt at dismissing them as paganistic acts. After a while he began to view his native land in a different light. He realised in a subtle way that the system in which he had spent most of his impressionable years, had inadvertently influenced him to look down on everything that he represented, resulting in him not appreciating himself and not realising it. It brought it home to him how inappropriate and quite incorrect the view he originally had of himself and his people was.

How living in Ghana impacted on his life

Ghanaian/African culture, traditions and heritage filled in so many crucial areas of his life that Tetteh had completely missed out on. In so many ways, that experience helped him to find himself. It gave him a better, clearer and more realistic sense of himself and his identity which led to a sharper focus on his renewed sense of direction.

Our life together as a couple
Difficulty with conception

Due to difficulty with conception after five years of marriage, we started to consider other options. Adoption rated very highly on our list. But, uncertain as to how to proceed, where to go and how to begin the process, we shelved the idea.

How we decided on adoption
Later on, long-lost friends of mine came to one of our summer barbecues with their children (the best behaved children I had ever met). To our surprise, not only were the two brothers and sisters adopted, but they were not siblings by birth either, and yet they all got on so well. Impressed and encouraged by them, we asked their parents how to proceed with adoption. Thanks to this wonderful turn of events, we began to feel optimistic about the prospects of adoption. By coincidence, our friends had adopted all their children in my local borough so the contacts proved to be straightforward. As it turned out, their Irish link worker became ours.

Adoption preparation
Adoption training course
As a couple seeking to adopt, we were invited after our application to go on an adoption training course, during which we learnt a lot, though not enough, about adoption. The course clarified a lot of myths and misconceptions about adoption in general, especially as I had always, rather naively, thought that the only children ever up for adoption were orphans.

Our motivation for adopting children
The circumstances under which children enter permanent care came as a real shock and could either have put us off or firmed up our resolve to carry on. It was a very good starting point because we realised how little we knew about adoption. Issues such as "contact with birth family" still unnerved us and we secretly hoped it would never come to that in our case.

Most of our initial fears and apprehensions were somewhat alleviated. If we did have any doubts at all at that stage, the sheer horror of statistics highlighting the disproportionately high number of black children in the care system made us feel it was our duty to carry on, having come this far. Our confidence was not so much in our ability as parents (because we were willing to learn) but what we felt capable of dealing with, once we had established with the social workers what our preferences were in terms of dealing with problems such as sexual abuse, disabilities and so on.

Finding the children

Although our initial preference was for a boy, we changed our minds to twins when we visited friends of ours who had recently had twins (boy and girl). They related so well and only had the most loving smiles for each other. We were smitten by the uniqueness of their relationship at the tender age of six months. I remember telling my husband on the way home how nice it would be if we adopted twins instead. We informed our social worker about our new decision.

Within a month, we saw an advertisement in *The Voice* newspaper for a two-and-a-half year old twin boy, Alan, and girl, Amy of Caribbean heritage, whose photographs touched something inside of us for different reasons. Amy looked just like one of my cousins would have looked at her age and Alan reminded me of an old family friend. My husband just liked what he sensed from the picture.

We immediately proceeded to make the necessary application through our link worker and finally, although ten other families applied to adopt the twins, we were selected.

First meeting with foster carer and family placement team
Foster carer's profile on twins

A meeting with all parties concerned including the children's white foster carer was the biggest eye opener of all. The foster carer's profile on the children was a long list of gross and outrageous behaviour which seemed rather extreme for two-year-olds but it had to be true or she would not have been telling us.

The twins terrorised other children so much that other parents kept and protected their children from them. They had been expelled from their first nursery school at two years of age and their foster carer had been unable to find another nursery that was willing to admit them. They were uncontrollably violent and destroyed everything in sight. She had had to put everything out of sight and out of reach. They only liked bananas and refused to eat with cutlery. They were very manipulative. Whenever she tried to pull him up for naughty behaviour, Alan would say with the most irresistible and charming smile, 'Kiss, kiss, Tina', and she would buckle and give in to kissing him instead.

One of the few goods things the foster carer said about the twins was that they were lovely children. They were lively and good at football. All of this was said with an assumption that that would be no more than we expected.

Effect of foster carer's profile of twins on me
The foster carer's judgement of the twins seemed too strong for children of that age. The possibility that, in two years of a human being's life, they could have developed such an advanced level of misbehaviour frankly scared me. Yet I had no reason to disbelieve her. After all, she was a very experienced foster carer who had fostered many different types of children including a few other black children for over 10 years with the same local authority.

Although she tried to inject hope and optimism by saying that the twins were lovely children who liked bananas and were good at football, I could not shake off my shock, horror and deep disappointment. I could not wait to get out of the meeting and be done with it. I had made up my mind. I was not going ahead with this adoption and that was that.

Never having heard of or imagined that two-year-olds could possibly be as bad as she described, I did not see how I could work with or manage children like that, with my relatively limited experience from the parenting point of view.

Effect of foster carer's profile of twins on my husband
Through my husband's experience in the English public school system, he had become aware of the stigmatisation and negative stereotyping that black children in England could be faced with – a view which resulted from persistent misperceptions and misunderstandings. He felt that the harshness of the foster carer's profile could be imputed to the preconceived negative perceptions of black people in general held by many ignorant white people. Notice her emphasis on the children's love of bananas and only eating with their fingers.

Her resignation and acceptance of the twins' bad behaviour and never really attempting to effectively correct them clearly illustrated the fact that she believed that it was only natural (i.e. it is in the nature of black people) for them to be outrageously behaved. My difficulty was that even children, innocent and uninformed as they were, could not even escape unkind perceptions and baseless reactions to such unfounded judgements.

Should we or shouldn't we go ahead with the adoption?
My husband finally managed to convince me that we go ahead and so I went along with the decision as a challenge. In spite of seeing it as a challenge I was still a trifle apprehensive about what possible input I could make to their lives to turn them around, if it was indeed possible especially considering that there could be some truth in the foster carer's assessment of them.

Background of the children
Brief life with birth mother
The children had lived with their birth mother up to the age of 1 year and 10 months. She had become quite ill through alcohol abuse and took them to the social services because she was no longer able to look after them.

Placement with white foster carer
The twins were immediately placed with Tina, their white foster carer, who lived with her husband, two daughters and two sons (whose ages ranged from 9 to 15 years). The twins were the only foster children in the household for 10 months until they moved in with us at two-and-a-half years of age.

Paediatricians's prognosis of the twins
They were docile and inactive, both behind their developmental milestones, and still crawling at 1 year 10 months. They could not talk at all. The social services' paediatrician said they would have a relatively retarded progress in life and would always be about two years behind their peers.

Meeting the twins
Coming face-to-face with the reality of becoming new parents
After we had found out that we were the lucky couple selected to adopt the twins, we were overjoyed. Lots of mixed feelings set in as the reality

drew nearer. After every stage of joy, I experienced feelings of apprehension wondering whether I had what it takes to be a mother. Thoughts of how different our lives would be kept coming to mind as I remembered the children who visited us. They all, thankfully, went back home to their parents and never got to the stage where they would outstay their welcome.

Our introduction to the twins
We had a two week period of introduction before the moving in date, where we saw the children almost every other day and filled the days in between with monosyllabic phone calls. We had sent photographs of ourselves and a few members of our family which the foster carer used effectively in introducing us to the children.

The twins' reactions to us
The foster carer did a marvellous introductory job because the children recognised us on sight. We had asked that they call us Daddy and Mummy which they did immediately. It was such a shock when they called me Mummy for the first time and it took me a while to get used to it.

Both children took to my husband immediately. Amy was quite open towards me though Alan was very guarded in his approach. Alan refused to have anything to do with me except approach me suspiciously and collect his gift from me. He remained guarded in his approach to me until about two weeks after they had moved in.

Separation and loss
Alan had had a particularly close relationship with his foster mother and appeared not to want to be parted from her. On one occasion during the two week introduction period, the foster mother left them at home with me for 45 minutes. Although most of their toys, by this stage, had been moved to our house, Alan stood at the locked door and cried non-stop until the foster carer came back for them. He clung onto her for the rest of their stay calling her Mummy and refused to look in my direction or say goodbye when they were leaving. I felt hurt, rejected and confused as to why he refused to even try to get to know me. I was later reassured by the link worker that it was quite normal and was only a phase that some children went through when faced with the threat of separation and loss.

The twins' reaction to moving in with us
Our introductory programme worked out extremely well. Curiously enough, when the final day came for them to come home with us, the twins were ready to move. We were told that they had been up early and ready four hours before the appointed time and had spent a lot of time sitting on the doorstep waiting. When we arrived, we found them there with their suitcases and a huge box with a see-saw which their foster carer had bought them as a going away present.

Expectations versus confidence

Reality after moving in
The first two weeks after the twins had moved in were the roughest I have ever known in my life. To some extent they were just as their foster carer had described but not without reason as we were later to discover. It also struck home how easily and alarmingly one can be condemned when plausible explanations or reasons for such bad behaviour go unrecognised. Bad behaviour such as that displayed by the twins is only symptomatic of an imbalance or deeper emotional or psychological problem which children at that age are incapable of articulating in words. In the first place, children of that age lack the sophistication in compre-hension, language or vocabulary to communicate such complex issues and secondly, Alan and Amy's speech development was slow.

Uncontrollable and destructive
The placid and docile twins placed with the foster carer had received, in the 10 months with her, enough stimulation to make them over-active. The question was whether it was positive or negative stimulation. The twins were like ricocheting bullets and were totally uncontrollable. I could not turn my back on them for a moment or leave them in a room for a minute without something disastrous happening. The coat rail in the hall got ripped out of the wall. Our curtains, complete with curtain rail, came down. The freestanding wardrobe in their bedroom got broken, and if it had not been wedged between two beds, it would have fallen and possibly hurt them.

Very angry children

Books got ripped up into shreds. My make-up was smeared all over their faces, our bedroom walls, bed and carpet. It didn't take too long to realise that they were angry children. Their speech was delayed considerably and they had only just started saying their first few words not too long before they moved home with us. They could not really speak properly, yet their vocabulary was nearly all swear words which they used, surprisingly, in the right context.

Sending wrong messages to the children

Earlier on I mentioned how Alan would manipulate their foster carer into giving him a kiss after he had been naughty to avoid being told off. This particular act and lack of control was at the the root of a lot of the twins' bad behaviour especially in Alan's case. Amy, on the other hand, followed mischievously where her brother led and at times even exceeded him in naughty behaviour. They had learned inadvertently, especially Alan, to be rewarded for naughtiness. Sadly, it had happened unintentionally.

Hooks for love

Did we love them at the beginning?

At the beginning, I cannot honestly say that I loved them in the maternal sense of the word. I felt compassion towards them and cared very much for them. Their initial "raw" behaviour provided me with no hooks on which I could hang my coat of love. Later on, a hint of the beautiful side of their nature began to seep out.

The beautiful side of their nature seeps out

They loved plants and animals and appreciated beautiful things in nature like rivers, pebbles and, most especially, flowers which Alan would pick to give to his special friends. They would both do the same for me whenever their daddy took them out without me.

Purity of their forgiving nature

Watching them play in the garden three days after they had arrived and during the period of the general tearing down of the house, Alan got off his bike momentarily to admire a flower when his sister Amy got off her bike and started riding Alan's. He rushed back for his bike begging, kicking and screaming for the unperturbed sister to give him back his bike. After a while of him not giving up and she not giving in, she suddenly got off his bike.

He rushed to get on his bike before she changed her mind. But even before the last tear could fall on his cheek, he turned sweetly to his sister and invited her to join him on his bike so they could ride together. She shamelessly obliged and the two rode together happily for the rest of the afternoon. My heart absolutely melted.

Found my hooks for love
If, at any point, I had become discouraged by the chaos and broken furniture around us, this made me feel hopeful again and gave me the extra incentive to carry on with the adoption. These pure acts which stemmed from the children's inner beauty – which every child has, even the most monstrous of them all – provided the hooks on which my love now overflows.

Our initial approach to getting to know the children
Observing the twins to start with
We had both decided that we would spend the first two weeks just watching and observing the twins to get to know them and also allow them the space to get used to us and their new environment. Being inexperienced as parents we would learn how best to relate to them by observing their interaction with each other. We had also been warned by the social workers to expect a lot of playing up and they suggested that we try the gentle, tolerant, softly-softly approach in order to not alienate them.

Attention seeking for the wrong reasons
Our twins demanded attention at any cost be it good or bad and would do anything for attention. They did outrageous things to be noticed, because somehow the attention and disapproving responses they got made their day. They preferred negative attention. We soon realised that reactions of anger, outrage, disbelief and sheer horror at something they

had done wrong amused them because being told off made no impact on them whatsoever.

Disliked themselves

It became quite clear to us that the twins at such a tender age had become victims of harsh prejudgements which they had come to believe and accept. Inevitably, it had become a self-fulfilling prophecy, resulting in the distortion of their personality and the low self-esteem that makes self-destruction more likely.

We finally realised that the basis of a lot of their bad behaviour could be imputed to their lack of self-love and self-respect which had resulted from the influence of their environment.

How we managed bad behaviour

Failure of our softly-softly approach

The twins lacked any form of discipline or structure. They had no conception of boundaries or limits so they did as they pleased. After the first four days, the house was virtually unrecognisable and things were not getting any better. They were now beginning to manipulate us and our softly-softly attempts at correcting them was proving to be more ineffective as they became more defiant.

Negative response to praise

Praises meant nothing to them because they did not like themselves. Soon after you had given them a good dose of praise, they would turn around and do something quite shocking, like breaking a toy or destroying something.

Unfortunately, three years on, Alan's problem of "praise-worthlessness" surfaces every now and then at school but on a relatively minor scale. It is an ongoing battle which we are still working on in conjunction with the white female class teacher. Although we have only had four such instances in the last year at school, it is a real area of concern because of its wider implications.

The methods we found effective – drawing from past experience
We realised that allowing this wanton destructiveness to continue was not only irresponsible but was potentially very dangerous for all of us. We tried several methods of controlling their behaviour and finally, the only resource that proved effective was drawing from my past experience on how our parents had managed our naughty behaviour. We decided to take the matter into our own hands and became stern and intolerant of any bad behaviour.

Routine
We established a realistic routine for the twins as soon as they moved in and that helped them develop a sense of belonging. Soon they were pre-empting our next moves which also made them feel they were in control of their lives.

Tailoring disciplinary measures to suit their personalities
Having studied them, in those few chaotic days, we realised the need to tailor the discipline and punishment to suit their personalities which fortunately were very similar at the time.

Time out
Simply telling them off had failed so the best approach had to involve some kind of action. We came up with "time-out". The children's initial reaction was one of disbelief as the threats of doing time-out were enforced.

Any misbehaviour landed them in the naughty corner (with a clear explanation of why we were sending them there) where they would be made to sit silently and simply watch passively as we carried on with an exciting activity that they loved. They were forbidden to participate and this proved to be very effective because they hated to be tied down or be left out of any activity that involved other people.

A slightly more severe punishment was doing time-out by the stairs with their hands behind them facing the wall, where there was nothing to play with or destroy. Every five or ten minutes, they were summoned to explain why they were being punished and they, in turn, had to tell us what lesson they had learnt from it. If they couldn't explain it, they were sent right back.

Positive discipline

If they tore a book, out came the sellotape for them to put it back together. It did not matter how grudgingly they did it, or how long it took, all we wanted was to see their attempt at undoing their wrong behaviour. In putting the onus on them to correct their own undoings, they started developing a sense of responsibility towards their actions and beginning to respect their environment.

Effect of setting limits and boundaries

It was a sobering period in the children's lives. We did not allow them to get away with anything we were aware of. This method worked very well with the twins because it began to introduce some discipline into the way the twins managed things. It controlled their defiance because we were consistent and became very firm with them. It ended up not only teaching them right from wrong and being responsible but the time-out discipline, surprisingly, helped to improve their speech as they were forced to express themselves quickly to be released.

Action-packed praise

We actively demonstrated the beauty of praise by following it up with a treat like going to the shops and, if they had been really good, they were allowed to hand the money over at the counter and collect the change from the shopkeeper for goods bought. They might even be given their own little bags to carry home. Or it might be a trip to the park or helping mummy cook. We made sure that the dangling carrots were always day-to-day outdoor activities which we could carry out immediately. They love the outdoors and by this approach going out was elevated to a big treat for them.

Constructive punitive play

The naughty child was left behind with one of us, with a single toy, if he or she was lucky and they were made to play with that toy (mainly bricks or lego) alone, or not at all. The twins lacked a sense of focus and concentration so this discipline forced them to do just that. Soon Alan (the naughtier of the two) was making the most fascinating and interesting constructions. We recognised the possibility that if he equated punishment with too much lego and bricks he may grow up to hate them. To eliminate that possibility, we would reward each ingenious construction with a photo shoot of him behind his masterpiece after he had satisfactorily explained his behaviour.

Developing pride in their own creation

After those sessions, one could actually see him expanding with pride and a sense of self-worth which was illustrated by how proudly he showed off his masterpiece to his sister who would immediately want to do a similar one for us to admire and take a photo of. This was to start them on their road to a more fulfilling approach to their lives in developing the concentration and focusing needed to get by, especially at school.

Our mode of communicating with the children

We had a policy of not talking in baby language to the children even when they came out with so little vocabulary. In Ghana it is believed that the best time to get through to people is when they are babies and very young. It was quite amazing to observe how rapidly the children's articulation progressed through the explanations of their behaviour, word for word, just as it had been explained to them. They (especially Alan) now have a wonderful ability to quickly memorise poems, books, quotations (after hearing them once) accurately.

Teaching them appropriate use of language

As to the swearing, we explained to them fundamentally how rude and inappropriate it was and asked them not to use any of those expressions again. It failed at first but our new-found disciplinary regime soon took care of that. Within three days they had completely stopped swearing.

Relaxing the discipline as children's behaviour improved

Unfortunately this new disciplinary approach meant that our home had to be run like a military regime. We found that as time went by the children's behaviour had improved so much that we no longer needed to be so rigid.

Other behavioural disorders
Food and the twins
Yes, the children did like bananas but they also liked a whole lot of other foods too (West Indian, Chinese, Indian, Japanese and Italian) including taking to the rich variety of Ghanaian foods that we gradually introduced as their main diet at home.

Eating with cutlery and their fingers
The reason they ate with their fingers, we discovered, was because that was all they knew. They mastered the ability to use a spoon and fork in a day after we had showed them how. We also showed them the cultured way of eating properly with their fingers, which they needed to know for those Ghanaian dishes that only taste better when eaten with the fingers, like fufu and kenke or dorkunu (as Jamaicans and the Akan speaking people of Ghana call it).

Inappropriate behaviour with white people
Kissing on the lips
Another expression of inappropriate behaviour was how they related to white people. They latched onto white people indiscriminately. I had lost Amy for a split second in a shopping centre and found her right behind me kissing an old white lady full on the lips.

Acting stupid for white people
Whenever they were with white people they would start acting stupid and do the silliest things. Suddenly they did not know the correct foot for their shoe, or would start to talk stupidly. It was almost as though they felt being stupid was the only way they would be acceptable to white people.

With such an attitude there cannot possibly be any hope for their future which would surely be grim considering that they will be dealing with white people in every facet of their lives, i.e. doctors, teachers, friends, etc. Something had to be done about it.

Children's pet-like interaction with white friends

Whenever white friends came to visit the twins would jump all over them. They were in and out of their hair and clothes in a ferret-like fashion whilst trying to involve the guests in the kind of games that people engage pets in. We could not stop them because they were so absorbed by their indulgence.

We thought that surely the best way to deal with this would be to ban all our white friends from coming to the house for a while until we had worked this out. But it was not possible because we had an open house.

Finally we decided to put the responsibility of correcting this habit in the hands of our white friends when they came to the house. We told them the type of behaviour we expected of the children and asked then to stop the children firmly when they stepped out of line with an explanation as to why it was inappropriate behaviour. It worked.

We have a popular Ghanaian proverb that says, 'A mother may be the one who gives birth to children, but the responsibility of the children's upbringing rests with the community'. We have drawn a lot of inspiration from that proverb and from a lot of our beliefs.

We also actively discouraged all inappropriate behaviour of adults towards the children and put the onus of correcting and enforcing family discipline on all the adults we are associated with.

Gradually the twins are realising the value of appropriate behaviour at all times with people in general which is helping them develop their self-respect and respect for others. We often talk about them respecting themselves and discuss the kind of behaviour that leads to self-respect and earning respect from others.

Monkey gestures

The most disconcerting of all their unsociable behaviour was acting like monkeys – the way they stooped with hands dangling at their sides cocked in monkey fashion when they walked with slightly bandy legs; the way they ate with their fingers, gorging their food into their mouths. In excitement they would shriek with hands dropped up by their cheeks moving up and down making monkey signs as they laughed.

I wondered about that but couldn't work out how they had cultivated the habit, until they both told us in jest one day to look at how monkeys behave, which they proceeded to demonstrate, laughing. Sadly all they had done, unbeknown to them, was mimic their own gestures. It was only then that we realised that they may have been the butt of sick racist jokes which they had acted out enough times for them to have become a part of their expressions because they probably got good laughs from it. Once again, this was another example where these vulnerable children had fallen prey to negative attention and taunts to their detriment.

Because we did not laugh at or encourage that sick joke they realised something was not right about it. It made it easier to point out to them what was wrong about it. We spent the next week re-educating and teaching them more sociably acceptable ways of expressing themselves. Having understood it they both worked at it and soon their expressions reverted back to normal.

The tragedy about this situation is that if this abnormal behaviour had carried on undetected, the children would have grown up with it, making them the butt of sick and painful jokes in their adolescence.

Fear of black people

Driving down the roads we frequently noticed that the children had a blind spot where black people were concerned. They saw and made comments only about white people. I thought nothing of it until I took them to one of the large department stores two weeks after they had moved in. They fled in hysterics from all the black sales ladies who approached to admire them and ran for protection, not to me, their mother, but to the other white sales ladies in the store. I managed to wrench them away from the scene to the nearest toilet to compose myself, and in a pathetic attempt to redress the situation, I insisted that they go back and shake hands with the first black sales lady they saw as we came out. They were both so petrified and shook so much that they were unable to extend their hands. Then I realised something was wrong.

Managing their fear of black people

To deal with the problem, we started buying them children's books with black characters, and their TV viewing was limited to the Cosby Show, Sesame Street and any other children's programmes with black casts. We told them stories about our childhood complete with photographs of the characters in the hope that it would help them to appreciate their own kind. We realised the importance of not forcing it down their throats as would have been the case if it was structured. It happened naturally because it is part of our lifestyle anyway. We also started taking them to more African and Caribbean shows and functions. We actively entertained more of our African, Caribbean and African-American friends and their children at home.

Gradually, without our realising it, they had actually started identifying themselves, not only with the children of the Cosby Show, but also little African children running around naked in the bush on TV. When the latter took place I wept for joy at the realisation that the twins were at last beginning to accept and appreciate themselves just for what they are. They could not understand why I suddenly hugged and kissed them laughing and crying at the same time. How could I explain such a difficult concept to them? I simply told them they were beautiful. To get this far was such a personal victory. It was undoubtedly one of the main highlights in our life with the twins.

The twin's first trip to Ghana
How they were received by the Ghanaian extended family
My father passed away a year after the twins had moved in so I went with them to Ghana. They were at one with the country and slotted so well into the system that the family were pleasantly surprised. A ceremony followed by a party was held for them, as is traditional, to officially welcome them into the family. They got to meet all the relevant members of the family because everyone was there for my father's funeral.

How the twins related to being in an African country
Fortunately, all the cousins in the house were their age group. They enjoyed seeing so many black people in one place, a reality that was completely new to them. They felt safe. They enjoyed the beaches and seeing various reptiles and animals all over the place such as lizards, chickens, frogs, goats, etc. They developed an even greater sense of belonging and knew instinctively that this was their home too. They related very well to everything there without question or reservation. The trip was one big adventure for them and impacted so much on their

lives that their memory of the trip is as fresh today as it was then. They loved Ghana so much they did not want to come back to England. On the day of our departure they hid under their beds in the hope that we would leave them behind if we could not find them.

The children recognised the difference between England and Ghana and yet accepted it whole-heartedly. That experience was so reassuring for me because it proved that they had accepted us and where we come from, having effortlessly related so well to our home country.

Conclusion

The big issue for black carers and adopters is that many of the black children in transracial placements do not have positive messages given to them by their white carers or agency about black families. This is a very important issue that needs to be addressed for such placements to work. One can understand the problems that arise in the final placement of a child who has had several moves. But in the case of children who have had only one or two moves, there should not be a big issue about helping them move on to more appropriate placements. When a child has had a positive attachment in an environment where negative images about their heritage and culture have been actively discouraged and where they have been fed with positive messages about their culture to encourage a better sense of self-esteem and self-worth, then the final placement of the child stands a better chance of succeeding and becoming permanent.

10 Transracial placements: an adoptee's perspective

Sue Jardine

Introduction

Drawing on my own experiences of being transracially adopted, I will address three main issues: loss, racism and identity. These factors have had a profound impact on how I have developed my sense of self. It is only because I have, as an adult, worked through much of the pain I experienced while I was growing up, that I can write about it clearly now. The understanding I have of myself and my adoption has been made possible through counselling and sharing experiences with other adults who have been transracially adopted. Validation of my experiences by other transracially adopted adults has occurred within the last five years, yet I have lived in this country for over thirty. The reason I have taken so long to express my feelings is because for most of my life I did not wish to be associated with my adopted status. For a long time I had great difficulty saying that I was adopted. It was a label that had negative connotations.

Impact of transracial adoption

Adoption meant I had been abandoned, adoption meant I had no roots, adoption meant that I was different, and adoption meant that I could not express the pains of my losses because I was too young to understand what had happened to me.

Openness in adoption is a new concept. The importance of personal history, birth family and ethnic origins was not considered at the time of my adoption; little thought was given to the fact that a baby may suffer from having being relinquished by her birth mother. The baby was integrated into the new family without any recognition that separation from her birth family may leave her emotionally traumatised. In addition, with regard to transracial adoptions, no consideration was given to how the baby may be viewed by society while growing up.

My adoptive parents have done the best they could for me, and in no way do I underestimate or undervalue the love they have given me. There is no doubt that, in terms of educational achievement and employment, my assimilation into this society has been very successful. However, it is necessary to look beyond these factors as indicators of adoption success, and acknowledge the emotional costs which I have borne as a result of being transracially adopted.

I was adopted in the 1960s from Hong Kong and was nearly 18 months old when I arrived in the UK. For a long time I have known that there would be little possibility of tracing my birth parents as I was found in Hong Kong without any identification on me. Apparently efforts were made to trace my parents when I was found but no one came forward.

Although I do not remember the initial separation from my birth mother the experience has had devastating consequences for how I perceive my sense of self and how I have dealt with relationships. As a child I assumed the blame for what had happened to me, and grew up in the belief that I must have been "bad" – why else would I have been given up for adoption? To be told I was relinquished out of love to give me a better life, put me in a position where love is equated with loss. The message I internalised was that to love would be to take the risk of being rejected again, something that I definitely did not want to happen. I was also under the impression that I might have died had I not been rescued, so at a very early age I knew that I should be grateful for being adopted. As a child, being told I was chosen and special left me wondering why my birth parents didn't keep me. At a very early age, my security was taken away from me and in my mind there were conflicting messages about why I was born and whether I was wanted.

Limited information and the lack of importance attributed to birth origins meant that, although I was told of my adoption at an early age, the subject was not spoken of again by my adoptive parents. I was given to understand that I knew all there was to know, which was very little. Not feeling able to ask my adoptive parents about my origins has meant I have had to absorb the burden of my losses, without actually understanding quite what those losses were.

I look in the mirror and see a face. It is that of a Chinese adult. I have no idea as to where it came from, who it was born to, or what characteristics I share with my birth family. So many questions unanswered. It is very painful to see others in family photographs which clearly display traits passed on through the generations. For me, it is such an alien concept to think that there must be other people somewhere, dead or alive, that are part of me, and me of them.

While I was growing up there were no opportunities for me to express openly my feelings about being given up by my birth parents. At times of separation, particularly deaths, I have felt devastated but had to contain my feelings. To let them out would have been too much for me to cope with. I have felt envious and angry that other people have had a ritual through which they could express their grief, envious that they had someone they knew they were grieving for, and envious that they were, as far as I could see, supported during their mourning. My losses are not tangible, so they do not exist.

Being adopted has left me with an overwhelming sense of being incomplete and being transracially adopted has meant that from a young age I have had to grow up knowing that I was different to the people around me.

Growing up in a family where I was obviously different from the other members, and under circumstances where I did not know anything about my origins, left me feeling very vulnerable. At a very young age it was necessary for me to explain my status, despite the fact that I did not understand it myself. I felt stigmatised by not having my own birth family history and I felt that I had to justify my existence.

Understandably I developed an acute sensitivity to my lack of roots and history because the majority of people, who are not adopted, take their family situations for granted. At school, exercises such as drawing a family tree, or finding where my adopted family surname came from did not sit comfortably with me. Other occasions which I have found difficult are weddings or observing family reactions to births because yet again they are harsh reminders of my abandonment and the fact that I look different from the rest of my family.

In addition to absorbing the losses associated with my adoption, my assimilation into a white family has meant that I have struggled with my sense of racial identity, that is, of being Chinese on the outside but growing up with the values and culture of an English white person.

Within my family I have always been regarded as being the same as my brothers and sisters, who are born to my adoptive parents. This approach to me, whilst well intended, could not remove the fact that this was not the case. My physical features betrayed me. Not only did they set me apart from my family, but they attracted attention I would rather not have had.

Not surprisingly I was unable to defend myself when racist comments were made about me because I couldn't relate to my Chinese self; I had no strength or pride in having Chinese origins. Although my adoptive parents told me that I should be proud of who I was, there were not enough positive Chinese images I could draw upon to reinforce their statement. It was not as if my adoptive parents had no contact or knowledge of Chinese people and Chinese culture; before I was born they lived in Singapore, and when I was at primary school we had a Chinese student living with us for a few years. The connections my family had with Chinese people were not enough to overcome my need to disassociate myself from Chinese people.

Strategies for dealing with being transracially adopted

The ways in which I coped with being transracially adopted took four main forms.

Denial

Being able to bury my losses and to deny my difference was a very powerful way in which I protected myself. I was just Sue. I was not Sue who is adopted, or Sue the Chinese girl, or Sue Jardine with the Scottish surname and family who look different to her, but just Sue. I was resistant to giving myself labels and I did not appreciate being labelled.

Avoidance

I have never found it difficult to initiate relationships because I always volunteered myself as the "listener". This enabled me to avoid talking about myself or my family. I became very skilled at evading questions about myself.

In order to cope with racism I tried to avoid situations where I might be open to abuse. Of course I could not always anticipate these times, and racism is not always so blatant as name calling.

I also made sure I kept my distance from Chinese people. I looked too much like them. The fact that we had a Chinese student staying in our house while I was growing up did not help me to acknowledge my Chinese origins. It resulted in me feeling more confused about how I looked and where I fitted in.

The fact that I cannot speak any Chinese language was another reason why I avoided Chinese people. Not being able to understand the language has, at times, left me feeling extremely inadequate and embarrassed. When English people have greeted me in Chinese and I could not answer in the appropriate way, they have immediately made assumptions about my background. I have been told how sad it is that my parents have denied me my cultural roots (the belief being that I was raised by Chinese birth parents who have become too Westernised). If I do say I was adopted from overseas I have been told that I should learn Chinese. It is as if I am consciously denying my roots. There is no understanding or recognition of how difficult it is for me to take that step. It is humiliating and painful to be told what I "should" be.

Independence

Distancing in relationships protected me from being hurt or rejected. On the surface it appeared that I was very independent and in control. It took a long time for me to trust people and often when I did become close to someone I would test the relationship to the extent that it broke down. The need to sabotage relationships ensured I maintained control and reaffirmed my feelings of not being good enough. I would repeatedly experience feelings of rejection, even though I had set up the patterns in the first place.

Fitting in

Throughout my school years I was unaware that I was applying various different strategies to find a way of fitting in with my peers. At different times I either tried to be as invisible as possible, make every effort to please everyone so that I would not be attacked, or I became the class "fool". Adolescence is supposedly a time when young people experiment, become part of a peer group, test their parents and gain a sense of individuality. For me it was a time when I perfected my methods of survival. I felt unable to test my adoptive parents for fear of being rejected by them. For a long time I was leading a double life. In public I was extrovert and well adjusted but internally I felt isolated and inadequate.

As an adult I became increasingly aware that my strategies were not working. It was no longer possible for me to deny the fact that I am Chinese and adopted. Not being able to deal with this information prompted me to seek help.

Counselling/support

Through counselling I was able to address deeply buried feelings I have about being adopted. I no longer feel the need to deny my origins. Being able to voice my thoughts about my situation on a one-to-one basis gave me the strength to join a support group for transracially adopted adults, the Association for Transracially Adopted People (ATRAP).

The group was launched in October 1993 and evolved from discussion groups held at the Post Adoption Centre, London. There are over 80 adults in the group and the age range is from 19 years to over 40 years. For many members of the group, as for me, it was the first time we had met people with similar experiences to ourselves. Although our origins and family situations are diverse, we all share issues around loss, racism, and racial identity. From listening to other people's experiences and being able to voice my own I have come to realise how much, from an early age, we felt it was necessary for us to take responsibility for our adoptive status. This situation was perpetuated because many of us had grown up in isolation and we also felt we had to protect our adoptive families from having to deal with our experiences.

Seeking cultural identity

Through conversations with members of ATRAP who had either traced or were searching for their birth parents, I was able to see that it is not unnatural to want to know more about birth origins; I would not be betraying my adoptive parents by wanting to find out as much as I could about my racial identity. Initially I explored my Chinese self through activities such as reading books by Chinese authors, and going to Chinese films. However, it didn't take long for me to realise that knowing the history of a country or reading up on the culture is not a substitute for living and breathing it.

Attending a Chinese painting class run by the Chinese Community Centre in Soho, London enabled me to break down some of the barriers I felt about Chinese people. At the time painting was the only thing I felt able do with Chinese people because I could not speak Chinese. Although I warmed to the people in the class, I had again to explain my background. Being with Chinese people rekindled the pain I felt about not having my own birth family and I felt very self-conscious of being so English.

An important step for many adopted people to achieve some sense of identity is to trace their birth parents and, particularly in the case of people who are transracially adopted, to visit their country of origin. The nature of my adoption and the circumstances around my birth have meant that I have grown up with the belief that it is not possible to trace my birth parents. Because of this, and the feelings I have had towards Chinese people, it has taken me a long time to feel that I could visit Hong Kong, my birth place, and China, my cultural roots. In my fantasies I am embraced by my countries of origin and my birth parents will appear, and they will heal the pain of all that I have lost. Accepting reality is not easy.

My experience of visiting Hong Kong and China was both liberating and depressing at the same time. I felt liberated because I had made a connection with my racial origins by and for myself. I was in a position of being able to recall my own experiences of each country, in which, for the first time in my life, I felt I fitted in (at least physically) with the people that surrounded me. I was depressed because my link with Chinese people was and is, literally, surface deep. I felt saddened by the fact I could not speak a Chinese language, that I was a foreigner and that I was not, as was the case for many of the Chinese people on my flight, visiting family or relatives in Hong Kong and China.

The struggle for me to form a positive identity has not been easy. It is a struggle which, although I needed to do it for my self, I believe could have been easier if there had been certain policies and support systems in place at the time of my adoption.

What would have helped

Whilst family composition and dynamics have a significant impact on adoption success, I believe it is essential that both adoptive parents and professionals working with a family who have adopted a child from overseas, clearly understand that "race" and cultural heritage have a crucial role to play in terms of how the child forms a positive identity. In the light of this I would say that being adopted into a Chinese family would have been the best way of developing and supporting that need. As this was not available to me at the time of my adoption, drawing from my experience of being transracially adopted I would recommend support be given in the following ways:

- Adoptive parents being clear and honest about their motivations for adopting, for them to explore their own feelings of loss, and look at their attitudes towards the background of their adopted child. In the assessment process potential adopters would need to show that they recognise their own cultural identities, that they are aware of their attitudes towards difference, and that they can deal with the consequences of difference.
- Providing the child with as much information as possible about their origins and direct access to that information. Care and attention are required to ensure that the information collected by adoptive parents and professionals is accurate and does not take a Eurocentric view of the child's country of birth. If there are a number of agencies involved in the adoption process it is important that the information gathered is centralised. In my case three agencies were involved in my adoption. Despite the fact that I visited Hong Kong and China three years ago, it is only through my persistence that I have recently obtained vital information from Hong Kong regarding where I was found. When I initially approached the agencies involved, I was told that this information did not exist.
- Adoptive parents maintaining meaningful contact with birth parents and birth relatives when they are known to them.
- The adoptive family producing a life story book or video depicting the child's origins in a way which promotes a positive sense of racial origins and cultural heritage.
- Adoptive parents demonstrating their willingness to bridge the

cultural gap for the child by living and participating in communities which are multicultural, where there are people which reflect the child's origins. If I had lived among Chinese people I would have felt less isolated, I would have been more accepting of my physical looks, and it would have been more difficult for me to build up stereotyped views of Chinese people. Living among Chinese people would have also been a way in which I could have absorbed the language and cultural beliefs. Adoptive parents and professionals need to forge links with black and minority ethnic communities to show that they genuinely value the ethnic identity of the transracial adoptee. They also need to understand that cultural experiences cannot be replicated by occasional visits to the child's country of origin, or by attending festivals once a year. Token gestures can, in fact, be counter-productive and leave the child even more confused about their identity.

- Adoptive parents acknowledging racism and seeking schools with an anti-racist ethos. Professionals need to equip themselves and adoptive families with the skills to deal with racism so that the child feels confident that they can talk to their parents.
- Post-adoption services being available to the child as he or she grows up, and specifically targeting children/young people/adults adopted from overseas. When I was in need of help I did not approach post-adoption agencies because I thought their services were only for adoptees who were wishing to trace their birth parents and relatives. Discussion groups, such as those provided by post-adoption agencies, are invaluable for addressing issues and for putting adoptees in contact with one another. Being able to access a telephone helpline like TALKadoption (which opened in December 1997) would have also helped a great deal. The role of adoption agencies should not end when adoption is legally finalised. There is a great need for adoptees and adoptive families to have access to support and counselling if necessary, and for them not to feel stigmatised for seeking help.
- The adoptee having a buddy or mentor they can call upon if necessary, to explain about cultural festivals, to show them how to cook, or how to approach concerns such as hair or skin care. A resource centre, where adoptees can explore their cultural heritage and meet other adoptees, would also be of great value.

* * *

Some of the recommendations I have outlined above are standard practice but this is in no way universal. Because overseas adoption seems particularly hard to regulate it is not easy to evaluate the services available to adoptees and their families, and establish whether a commitment is being made by agencies and adoptive families to address the importance of racial identity and cultural heritage.

It is my sincere hope that this account aids understanding of the issues many transracially adopted people face while they are growing up. Adopted children want their adoption to succeed as much as adoptive parents and professionals, so it is in their "best interests" to do as much as they can to fit in. For transracially adopted children this is invariably done by denying their racial identity, and is often reinforced by adoptive parents, professionals, and the media who hold the view that "love is enough". As my experience illustrates, good intentions do not address the deep seated issues encountered by transracially adopted people.

I therefore call on professionals and prospective adopters to give due consideration to the fact that adopted children grow into adults who have enough loss to contend with (by virtue of the fact they are adopted) without having the additional loss of racial identity and cultural heritage.

11 Preparing young black people for leaving care

Lynda Ince

Introduction

The preparation of young black people leaving care is one of the most neglected areas in child care research. There are serious gaps in knowledge and understanding as to what precisely is needed in preparation work with young black people. The aim of this chapter is to focus on the relationship between "race", culture and identity as contributory factors in the ability of young people to cope successfully after discharge from the care system.

This chapter is derived from my M.Phil thesis in which I studied various levels of preparation and outcomes for ten young black care leavers (Ince, 1998). Leaving care in this context means discharge at the statutory leaving care age.

The implementation of Children Act 1989, section 22 (5) (c) (DoH, 1989) and the underlying principles of participation and working in partnership, if applied consistently, should assist in reducing power imbalances between professionals, and the family and young people. The young person's voice *must* be heard, and he or she be given every opportunity to fully participate in the decision making processes. In relation to leaving care, the Children Act 1989 gives guidance to local authorities under section 24 (1), 61 (1) and 64 (1) which gives strong messages regarding the need to prepare young people for independence. Macdonald (1991) notes that the Children Act 1989 under section 22 (5) (c) recognises the importance of race, culture, religion and language, and, that being the case, it must apply to *all* sections of the Act. The important question she posed was how these legal requirements would be dealt with in practice.

Previous research evidence on leaving care

The literature on leaving care has shown links between the care experience, lack of support, loneliness, lack of family ties, homelessness and unemployment. Past research has shown that leaving care is a formidable task for most young people (First Key, 1987; Bonnerjea, 1990; Stein and Frost, 1990; Broad, 1993). The lack of preparation in basic life skills has been reported in almost every study conducted. This type of research which discussed the experience and the process of leaving care began in the 1970s (Godek, 1976; Mulvey, 1977; Kahan, 1979; Lupton, 1985; Stein and Carey, 1986). In more recent years the work of Biehal *et al* (1995) and the Audit Commission (1994) have concentrated on the continuing difficulties which young people face after leaving care.

An investigation by First Key (1992), the national organisation for young people leaving care, highlighted considerable gaps in service delivery following the implementation of the Children Act 1989. A requirement to write policies for care leavers failed to be implemented nationally. A disparity between what different local authorities offered became evident. For example, First Key found that, out of 75 local authorities, 47 per cent had not complied with this requirement, 49 per cent did not offer after care support, 81 per cent had no written guidelines to give to care leavers, and only 35 per cent had produced written guidelines for social workers. First Key (1996) has since published a report of a national working group, recommending 17 standards for leaving care.

Young black people leaving care

It is striking that over a period of two decades of research little or no recognition has been given to the particular needs and experiences of young black people and that their position within the care system has been grossly neglected. Hence, limited knowledge exists about what happens to black children in the care system, in terms of preparation for leaving care or indeed what happens to them as young people in the post-care experience.

The work of the Commission for Racial Equality (CRE) in conjunction with First Key (1987) identified multiple problems faced by young black people. Similarly the work of a group of young black people,

Black and in Care, during 1984, gave evidence of deep-rooted problems faced by young black people in care. Biehal *et al* (1995) investigated leaving care schemes in three local authorities and were only able to identity nine young people identified as black, Asian or of mixed heritage. However, their study investigated "race", culture and identity and found that it was important for young black people in care to be given opportunities for exchange with people of "similar origins". Garnett (1992) documented similar findings, although her study did not specifically focus upon "race" and ethnicity. She found that half the young people in her study were of mixed heritage, and made mention in her findings of the many difficulties encountered by black young people leaving care. She acknowledged that 'young people from black and minority ethnic groups may be further disadvantaged as a result of being cared for within a predominantly white, ethnocentric care system'. She concluded that at best this system ignores "race", religion, culture and at worse it is 'overtly racist'.

The serious omission of young black people is addressed by Barn (1993) in her study of black children in the public care system. In relation to rehabilitation and discharge, she noted that mainstream studies have concentrated on white children and excluded black children from research analyses. Barn also found that several studies have commented on the over-representation of black and mixed heritage children in the care system without analysing reasons for this. It is equally true to say that there has been little or no attention given to their needs in terms of preparation for leaving care and support after leaving care.

Research findings

The section below highlights some significant findings from my qualitative study of ten young black people and draws implications for social work practice.

The sample consisted of ten young black people who had either left care or who were in the process of doing so. All of the study sample had been placed in long-term care in the early 1970s. Of the sample, six were female and four were male. All of the young people were of African or African-Caribbean origin with five being of mixed heritage, that is, with one black and one white parent.

1. Eurocentric care

Prolonged and extensive periods in care exposed all of the young people to a white Eurocentric model of care, with adverse implications for reintegration with their family and community. This was a key variable in their perceptions of themselves and their ability to cope after leaving care. Restricted contact with parents, relatives, black friends and the wider black community diminished the extent to which opportunities were presented for cultural exchange and conscious awareness of being black. The role of the black family in acting as a buffer and offering protection for the child from a hostile society is an extremely important one for black children living in Britain. The most legitimate form of self-awareness is the grounding of self in the history of one's family and community, but for the sample, this was missing. It is such a contextual grounding that was lacking within the care system, and which eventually damaged and distorted perceptions and self-awareness of these young black people.

The duration of their stay in the care system had serious repercussions. These only became evident at the stage of leaving care and when the young people had an opportunity to reflect on and review their life experiences. At the stage of leaving care, which is associated with the transition to adulthood and making adjustments to move away from a state of dependence to independence, these young people were experiencing turmoil. This is also a critical stage of development associated with psychological changes and puberty. Given support, this crisis can be overcome, but for young people in care the concept of "crisis" may last longer particularly for those who have lived in residential institutions. Residential establishments offering public care are characterised by a particular ethos in which there is a tendency to defer independence, and one which is not conducive to allowing young adults to test out their life skills or to make mistakes.

The young people in foster care had an advantage in that they were less fearful and had some ideas, however minimal, of how to survive after care. They also felt reassured that the placement would be open to them after leaving care. Clearly where this resource is made available to young people, it can significantly reduce feelings of loneliness and isolation. This made a marked difference to self-confidence and the ability to become independent and self-motivating. Nevertheless, the serious nature of the task that confronted them was not understood until they had left care and support systems were no longer available to them.

2. Disengagement from black family/community
Systematic denial of contact with those most likely to transfer cultural values was a recurrent theme in the stories that were recounted. The role of the family in transferring meanings, values, folkways, symbols and tradition were lost to those young people who were separated from their family of origin and community. This effectively dislocated the young people from any understanding of themselves and gave opportunity for negative value systems and confusion over racial identity to develop. The role of culture and its importance to young black people growing up in Britain was not well understood, and was always undermined as unimportant and without value. This led to suppression and denial of the importance of "race".

The young people had no personal attributes or strategies to resist the many states of powerlessness and oppression that were experienced. Lack of strong identification with family and relatives deprived them of opportunities to learn how to cook, how to care for their hair and skin, how to enjoy black art and history, and indeed how to feel proud about themselves. Those who entered the care system when they were older did not experience this problem. The study found that during the early years of reception into care there was little or no knowledge of the needs of black children. Assumptions were made that it was better to place children in white families than to leave them in residential care. Attempts to find black carers were extremely limited. Poor policy and practice had a deep impact upon the lives of black young people even after they had left the care system. Many of them still had vivid memories of what had occurred and how it had affected their present day abilities to cope.

The myth that black children do not want to be placed with black families must be vigorously challenged. This is an ideology that is all too often accepted without real consideration of the long-term effects of transracial placements. Local authorities must now pay attention to building up and recruiting consultants and experts who can work with black children and young people. They must consciously listen to the voices of black service users who are evaluating their experiences. In this research the young people said that, had they been placed in a black family from the onset of their care episode, this would have given them an opportunity to know more about and appreciate their "race" and culture. This type of work requires time, hard work and allocation of resources.

Identity stripping

This was a process defined as a method whereby racial and cultural needs were not met; racial identity was "stripped" through neglect and did more to serve the interests of professionals and white carers than the young people. It emerged as an important aspect of the care trajectory. Its impact on leaving care meant that many of the young people did not see themselves as black and felt ashamed of their colour. Transracial placements and environments where there were no reflections of black people reinforced identity stripping.

The research findings showed a failure amongst professionals and carers within fieldwork teams, residential and foster care settings to recognise and instil a positive representation of black reality. This occurred through the absence of positive images of the young people's racial origins and was a theme throughout their care experience. It was to be replicated over and over again. Many of the young people noted that no-one had ever sat down with them and discussed their "race" as a factor influencing their care experience. Lack of knowledge and under-standing of the importance of "race" and culture contributed to lack of promotion of the positive aspects of this part of the young people's identity. Consequently it was never actively discussed. One young person said:

No one ever said anything to me about my race.

Another said:

I've been in care for as long as I can remember, so it don't make no difference.

The inability on the part of staff and carers to discuss matters of "race" led the participants of this study to develop ambivalent feelings and lack of understanding about themselves. This resulted in the conclusion: 'I am white' or 'I am me'. One young man said:

I didn't understand the difference between colour. I thought there were no differences. I thought they were my mother and father. I thought that I was white.

To be brought up in care contributed to over-identification with white values and under-identification with their own "race", leading the respondents to separate themselves from other black people, at times being afraid of them. One young woman summed up this feeling by saying:

There was me going around thinking I was white, and then I realised I was not white ... I was scared of black people to be honest. I was scared of them, but now I know they are the same as everyone else.

The lack of attention given to the racial/cultural aspects of their lives in care rendered these black young people incapable of relating to black people. The loss of family and relatives reinforced loneliness and isolation in what one young person termed "the big wide world".

4. Overt/covert racism

All of the young people reported acts of racism of varying degrees from field work staff, residential staff, carers, peers and within the education system. In all of these instances the young people described the care system as "uncaring". The term uncaring was a word used by most of them to describe an activity that had a significant effect on preparation for leaving care and their perception of how others had devalued their existence.

Accounts were given of many incidents of unfair treatment, racism, oppression and discrimination within the care system that had devastating and long-term effects on their psychological development. A central theme in "non caring" was the neglect of racial and cultural needs:

Like if a member of staff was against you, you don't click, they would make life hard for you. They always say we care, but you know they don't really. There was a lot of that, it does hurt, it's not very nice.
and

You get stricter punishments than other people and things like that.
Other people done the same things, but some people just treat you
differently.
and
They would say we want to treat everyone equal, but we were not the
same at the end of the day. I had to start caring for myself when I was
young, they didn't care for me.

Behaviours that were attitudinal and covertly racist were denied, dis-owned or ignored, with the "perpetrator" going free and the youngsters suffering emotional damage. The young people reported racism within their home settings, which were by and large white and situated in isolated areas. In these environments they had to struggle against racist dogma and overt racist actions and often developed negative strategies to deal with with this. The psychological responses to racism are clearly documented in the research showing the methods and strategies developed by the young people as responses and coping mechanisms to deal with racism. These mechanisms were a chain of interconnected actions that are described in a model called "Making it Alone".

The Making it Alone model is very significant at the time of leaving care, when the young people described their struggles and their unpre-paredness for life after care. These processes were twofold: in the first instance, institutionalisation produced negative feelings and low self esteem about themselves; secondly, they felt alienated from their "race" and culture. It is important to realise that in the absence of positive black role models, all of the study sample reconstructed their internal worlds to idealise the people who were in many ways their oppressors by wanting to be white themselves or seeing themselves as individuals, but not *black* individuals. This was a way of making sense of their experi-ences and normalising inconsistencies. In so doing they moved along a continuum throughout the care process, fearful of challenging racism and always internalising negative concepts of themselves and others like themselves. An example of this is given in the following quote in which one young person used pejorative descriptions to express his views. These views replicated those of his carers who had a history of fostering Nigerian children through private fostering arrangements. The distinctions that are made stem from internalised negative attitudes, but are also a paternalistic response to those who are perceived as helpless and deserving of pity and charity. He described these views as "white" views and attributed them to where he had lived and the way he had been "brought up".

I've been brought up with white people, so I've missed a lot of cultural things. When I see coloured children on the telly in Ethiopia, I feel something. But when I see coloured people in London, and the way they act, I think some people got an attitude problem. I think, oh what the hell are they doing? I've got a lot of white views.

Analysis of the data revealed that such thinking prohibited the young people from understanding the nature of the black experience in Britain, and they absorbed negative racist views from those around them. The dilemma was the price that had to be paid for the transformation from black to "white".

Disruption in care

Movement and disruption were dominant features in the lives of some of the young people who had had several moves whilst in care. Barn *et al* (1997) found that African-Caribbean children spent lengthy periods in care, and that there was a strong correlation between length of stay in care and placement disruption (Barn, 1993). My study found that placement disruption led to a sense of rootlessness and instability, accompanied by an inability to achieve stability after leaving care.

The young people had also linked this to rejection regarding the way in which parents, professionals and carers had controlled them. This led them to feel a sense of powerlessness and an inability to write their own life script; they described feelings of rootlessness which they internalised as normal events. After leaving care, the feelings of rejection, separation and loss impinged heavily on their own ability to maintain stability and the problems remained unresolved.

Those who had achieved a stable foster placement or who had remained in their family until their teen years expressed more optimism about their ability to remain in their accommodation. Those who were in foster care or with relatives were also less troubled by instability since they were reassured that they could return to the family.

6. Educational needs

Educational needs were grossly neglected. Nine of the sample identified problems both at junior and secondary school. One said that she was helped only because there was a black teacher in her secondary school. Four were permanently excluded from school. Exclusion for long periods undoubtedly affected the young people's ability to achieve and to acquire a positive self-image. One young man came into care when he was one month old. He was excluded at age nine and drifted into crime. By the time of this research he was serving a long custodial sentence. Three males and two females in the study also had encounters with the police and left school without any qualifications.

Poor treatment within the educational system had a direct impact on the ability of the study sample to find employment after leaving care or to engage in further education. Failure in education also means an inability to become economically independent.

7. Life skills

The young people in the sample varied in the degree of help they had in acquiring practical life skills; only two had some help in independent units. Two others had gained some ideas from being in foster care. By and large the young people felt unequipped and with limited skills. In some instances the idea of "making it alone" was a burden. Individual responses from social workers showed that help received by the young people depended on the individual efforts of social workers. In such instances the young people described such acts as "caring". The general response, however, was that there was a lack of instruction or preparation for transition to adulthood.

No-one has come and talked to me and said you're leaving care on this day and this is happening. I know nothing, nothing at all about it.
and
I wasn't shown how to live my life.

Several years after leaving care one young person admitted:

I've only just in the last two years started literally to sit down with pen and pad to work my money out, whereas if I was prepared for that before, maybe I wouldn't be in as much money problems as I am now.

Without practical life skills it is impossible to cope. There were fears of having to make personal provision for needs and the youngsters experienced loneliness, boredom, poverty, and feelings of rejection and stigmatisation by the wider society. There were also concerns over managing money, caring for children, how to keep the house tidy, and generally how to survive. One young person said that he wanted help in knowing how to 'keep out of trouble with the law'. All of these factors became huge stumbling blocks for the respondents. The loss of family and a place in the black community also made them feel bereft of anyone to whom they could turn for help. These support systems were not readily available to them, except in the two instances where links had not been severed.

Implications for practice

The preparation for leaving care that young black people require should be based on a critical analysis of how "race" and culture impinge on the leaving care experience. Such an analysis shows that while it is important to provide training in life skills, more attention needs to be given to the individual and institutional acts of racism which can have long-term emotional and psychological effects on young black people. The experiences of the young people in the study showed that they had suffered some of the most appalling treatment not only as children in care, but as *black* children in care; this was revealed in the commentaries depicting events, people, language, treatment, actions and abuse of a physical and racial nature. Failure to encourage or instil a positive self-image was linked to the lack of contact with family and the systematic severing of ties with them and encouraging stronger links with white carers. To prepare young black people for leaving care, it is imperative that they have an understanding of their history and the positive achievements made by black people.

Making it Alone is a theoretical model which helps to understand the experiences of these young people and their individual coping strategies. It was linked to the feeling that no one "cared" and thus it became acceptable for them to become involved in crime, to stay out of school and generally fight their own battles. These strategies were unconscious and not recognised as harmful until the stage of leaving care. However, at this stage, Making it Alone became critical to independence and to survival, in that they had to fall back on their own inadequate resources to survive within the community.

In the absence of support systems, it is impossible for young people to cope with the trauma of leaving care. This study found that the notion of interdependence is central to preparation for leaving care; it recognises that all people find strength from an interconnected relationship with others. This is how true independence is eventually achieved. To enable this process, the local authority must first acknowledge its role in achieving an integrated approach to providing support through inclusion of parents, relatives, young people, carers, and all professionals involved with the child. This process should commence on a child entering the care system and be sustained throughout and beyond the care experience. Individual support for black children should include resources to enable identity work to take place.

For all black children and young people more support networks are required to sustain them through the care system. This means consciously building bridges across to the black community to encourage a more proactive role in recruiting black carers, volunteers, and "social aunts and uncles". The local authority must now regard this as a matter of urgency if the welfare of young black people is to be safeguarded, with the knowledge that long-term foster care in transracial placements in isolated geographic settings are not beneficial to the well-being of the black child.

The implications for practice have far-reaching consequences. It means that a new approach must be taken in developing strategies for working with black young people. Some specific aspects are listed below:

- The first and most crucial task is to acknowledge the impact of "race" and culture on preparation for leaving care.
- More attention must be given to providing placements that reflect the needs of black children and those which can offer positive role models.
- Black people should be represented at all levels of decision making within social services departments.

- More attention should be paid to the educational needs of black children.
- The need for advocates and independent visitors to act as representatives for young black people should be considered.
- Facilities should be provided for young people to test out living independently, make mistakes and be given support to do so.
- Skilled work on identity and helping young people to feel safe in exploring their racial origins and feeling a sense of pride should be offered.
- Racial harassment and abusive experiences both in the care and education systems must be tackled.
- There needs to be a restriction of placement of black children in geographical areas that are predominantly white.
- Preparation through life-skills development is central to preparation for leaving care.

Conclusion

The care system in Britain has a clear set of dynamics that do not work well for the black child. It was Booker T Washington who said:

The individual who can do something that the world wants done will, in the end, make his way regardless of his race.

"Race" should not be a stumbling block to receiving adequate and good enough care while children are being looked after by the local authority. They should be prepared as individuals who can do something well. This means giving them the tools of self-awareness to enable them to make positive choices, to avoid negative stereotyping and avoid "making it alone". In the struggle for liberation from an oppressive and controlling system, professionals need to reflect on their practice giving a more balanced analysis of the role and validity of cultural diversity. Such an analysis will enable young black people to fight for their rights not only on grounds of individualism, but also for customs, history, knowledge, music, food, friends, relatives, family and all the values that form the mosaic pattern of life. Starvation of these forms of cultural necessities has implications not only for the young person leaving care, but for the transmission of culture to their children and grandchildren in the ages to come. Expression of these will encourage young people to be more resourceful, to be less dependent on continuing state support and to reconstruct their lives in a major way.

The Children Act has replaced the term "in care" with "being looked after" but it will not significantly change the context of young people's experience unless there are major shifts in conceptual understanding. Such shifts will provide new impetus to provide good and positive black role models, and basic life skills from entry into care until the day they leave care. The role of the parent must be enacted at all stages of the care process and bridges must be built to accommodate working in partnership.

Thus, I conclude that preparation for leaving care must take on a new significance in the light of increased knowledge that is informed by research. Professionals must understand the implications for their actions and take responsibility for them. Moreover, professional competence will not be achieved unless clear structures and indicators are required of staff who work with black children and young people in the care system. Personal and institutional forms of discrimination and oppression should never be allowed to continue unchecked and without reparation.

References

Audit Commission (1994) *Seen But Not Heard*, London: HMSO.

Barn, R. (1993) *Black Children in the Public Care System*, London: BAAF/ Batsford.

Barn, R., Sinclair, R. and Ferdinand, D. (1997) *Acting on Principle*, London: BAAF.

Biehal, N., Clayden, J., Stein, M. and Wade, J. (1995) *Moving On*, London: HMSO.

Black and in Care (1984) *Black and in Care: Conference Report*, London: Children's Legal Centre.

Bonnerjea, L. (1990) *Leaving Care in London*, London: London Borough Regional Planning Committee.

Broad, B. (1993) *Improving Practice and Policy in Aftercare Work*: A Report of the National Children's Bureau Aftercare Consortium Conference, First Key.

Department of Health (1989) The Children Act 1989, London: HMSO.

First Key (1987) *A Study of Young Black People Leaving Care*, London: CRE.

First Key (1992) *A Survey of Local Authorities Provision for Young People Leaving Care*, London: First Key.

First Key (1996) *Standards in Leaving Care*: Report of the National Working Group, London: First Key.

Garnett, L. (1992) *Leaving Care and After*, National Children's Bureau.

Glaser, B. and Strauss, A. (1967) *The Discovery of Grounded Theory*, Aldine.

Godek, S. (1976) *Leaving Care*, Barnardo's Social Work Papers 2.

Ince, L. (1998) *Making It Alone*, London: BAAF.

Kahan, B. (1979) *Growing Up In Care*, Basil Blackwell.

Lupton, C. (1985) *Moving Out*, Social Services Research and Intelligence Unit Report, 12, Portsmouth Polytechnic.

Macdonald, S. (1991) *All Equal Under the Act*, Race Equality Unit.

Mulvey, T. (1977) *After Care Who Cares?*, Concern, no. 26.

Rickford, F. (1992) 'Moving On'. In *Social Work Today*, 2:5, pp 16–17.

Stein, M. and Carey, K. (1986) *Leaving Care*, Basil Blackwell.

Stein, M. and Frost, N. (1990) *Young People Leaving Care*, London: HMSO.

Strauss, B. and Corbin, J. (1990) *Basics of Qualitative Research: Grounded Theory, Procedures and Techniques*, Sage.

Appendix

Multicultural books and toy shops

Black Cultural Archives
378 Coldharbour Lane
London SW9 8LS
0171 738 4591

Centerprise Trust
136-138 Kingsland High St
London E8 2NS
0171 254 9632

Child's Play (Toy Shop)
18A Upper Tooting Road
London SW17 7PG
0181 672 6470

Commission For Racial Equality (CRE)
Information Section
Elliot House
10-12 Allington Street
London SW1E 5EH
0171 828 7022

Commonwealth Institute Resources Centre
230 Kensington High Street
London W8 6NQ
0171 603 4535

Early Years Trainers Anti-Racist Network (EYTARN)
77 Baker Street
Reading RG1 7XY
0118 939 4922

Equality Learning Centre
356 Holloway Road
London N7 6PA
0171 700 8127

Equality Street
Children's Marketing
Penguin Books
27 Wrights Lane
London W8 5TZ
0171 416 3000

Head Start (Books)
25 West Green Rd
London N15 5BX
0181 802 2838

Letterbox Library
Unit 2D, Leroy House
436 Essex Road
London N1 3QP
0171 226 1633

Mantra Publishing
5 Alexander Grove
London N12 8NU
0181 445 5123

New Beacon Book Shop
76 Stroud Green Rd
London N14 2DA
0171 272 4889

Oxfam Education Department
274 Banbury Road
Oxford OX2 7DZ
01865 311 311

Tamarind Ltd
P.O.Box 52
Northwood
Middlesex
HA6 1UN
0181 866 8808

The Working Group against Racism in Children's Resources (WGARCR)
460 Wandsworth Road
London SW8 3LX
0171 627 4594

Notes about the contributors

Sally Baffour is an adoptive parent to two young African children. She serves on the Black Perspectives Advisory Committee for the British Agencies for Adoption and Fostering (BAAF).

Nick Banks is a Lecturer in Social Work and a Chartered Clinical Psychologist at the Department of Social Work, University of Birmingham. He has taken a keen interest in adoption, fostering, contact issues, child development and identity work. He is of "mixed race" origin and has a particular interest in work with "mixed race" children and families. As well as academic work he continues in clinical practice and often appears as an expert witness in court. He is also involved in training practitioners in direct identity work with children.

Ravinder Barn is Senior Lecturer in Applied Social Studies in the Department of Social and Political Science, Royal Holloway, University of London. She has researched and published widely into the situation of black children looked after by local authorities. Her major publications include *Black Children in the Public Care System*, BAAF/Batsford and *Acting on Principle*, BAAF.

Bharti Dhir is Team Manager in a Children and Families team in the London Borough of Hammersmith and Fulham. She has extensive experience in the area of social work with families and children. Bharti has also been involved in training on Anti-Discriminatory Practice in Child Protection, Children with Disabilities, and Impact of Sexual Abuse on Black Identity.

Aminah Husain Sumpton was born in New Delhi, India and has lived in Egypt, Switzerland, and since 1970, in the UK. After her studies in psychology and social science at London and Surrey Universities, she qualified as a social worker in 1976. Her experience in the child care field includes residential child care, adoption and fostering, and as a guardian *ad litem*. Recently, her work as a child care consultant has involved training of lawyers, social workers and guardians, especially in child care matters, adoption, black children's particular needs and aspects of Muslim and Asian cultures.

Lynda Ince is a Lecturer on the Diploma in Social Work and also works for the London Borough of Harrow as an Independent Reviewing Officer. She completed her M.Phil at Brunel University writing her research thesis on the retrospective experiences of black young people in the care system. Her book, *Making it Alone*, was published by BAAF last year.

Sue Jardine is an Information Officer at the National Institute for Social Work (NISW). She is a member of the Association for Transracially Adopted People (ATRAP) and on the Management Committee of the Chinese Information Advice Centre, London. She has contributed to workshops, seminars and conferences on issues relating to transracial/ intercountry adoption and is committed to dispelling the notion that "love is enough" in transracial placements. It is her belief that existing research into transracial adoption and the presentation of the issues in the media are very limited and selective, and that there is a great need for the balance to be redressed. To that end she is currently involved in producing a video and piloting a research project looking at experiences of transracially adopted and long-term fostered adults.

Michael Mallows is a UKCP registered Psychotherapist with over 10 years post-adoption work counselling experience. He has also been engaged in training professionals who may come into contact with adopted and fostered youngsters. Former head of an adolescent therapeutic unit, Michael has helped design group programmes in exclusion units and created successful mentoring schemes in schools.

Toyin Okitikpi is a Lecturer in Social Work at Brunel University, London. He is currently completing a Ph.D. on inter-racial relationships.

He has a wide range of experience in social work, particularly working with children and young people. His interests include education; children, young people and crime; and inter-racial families.

Beverley Prevatt Goldstein is a Lecturer in the Centre for Applied Social Studies at the University of Durham. She currently directs the DipSW/MA programme and is also active in the management of Kemet, the Black Practice Learning Centre. She has considerable social work experience in child care, particularly in adoption and fostering. Her teaching, research interests and publications centre on identity, anti-oppressive practice, social work education, professional development of black students and the voluntary sector.

Alice Sawyerr is a UKCP registered Family and Systemic Psychotherapist at The Marlborough Family Service in London. She is also a visiting Lecturer in Family Therapy at Royal Holloway, University of London.